Nelson Advanced Science

Electricity and Thermal Physics

revised edition

Mark Ellse • Chris Honeywill

Endorsed by

edexcel

First published in 2000 by:
Nelson Thornes Ltd
Delta Place
27 Bath Road
CHELTENHAM
GL53 7TH
United Kingdom

This edition published in 2004

06 07 08 / 10 9 8 7 6 5 4

A catalogue record for this book is available from the British Library

ISBN 0 7487 7663 X

Illustrations by Hardlines and Wearset Ltd
Page make-up by Hardlines and Wearset Ltd

Printed and bound in Croatia by Zrinski

Contents

Option Topics

Introduction

This series has been written by Principal Examiners and others involved directly with the development of the Edexcel Advanced Subsidiary (AS) and Advanced (A) GCE Physics specifications.

Electricity and Thermal Physics is one of four books in the Nelson Advanced Science (NAS) series developed by updating and reorganising the material from the Nelson Advanced Modular Science (NAMS) books to align with the requirements of the Edexcel specifications from September 2000. The books will also be useful for other AS and Advanced courses.

Electricity and Thermal Physics provides coverage of Unit 2 of the Edexcel specification. Within this book are also the four option topics—Astrophysics, Solid Materials, Nuclear and Particle Physics, and Medical Physics – which, together with the AS practical examination, make up Unit 3 of the Edexcel specification.

Other resources in this series

NAS Teachers' Guide for AS and A Physics provides a proposed teaching scheme together with practical support and answers to all the practice and assessment questions provided in *Mechanics and Radioactivity*; *Electricity and Thermal Physics*; *Waves and Our Universe*; and *Fields, Forces and Synthesis*.

NAS Physics Experiment Sheets 2nd edition by Adrian Watt provides a bank of practical experiments that align with the NAS Physics series. They give step-by-step instructions for each practical provided and include notes for teachers and technicians.

NAS Make the Grade in AS and A Physics is a revision guide for students. It has been written to be used in conjunction with the other books in this series. It helps students to develop strategies for learning and revision, to check their knowledge and understanding and to practise the skills required for tackling assessment questions.

Acknowledgements

John Warren and David Hartley painstakingly read through and commented in detail on the manuscripts of the first edition. The authors and publishers gratefully acknowledge their major contributions to the success of the whole series. David Hartley also wrote the Nuclear and Particle Physics topic.
Mark Burton and Frances Kirkman gave kind assisstance during the preparation of the new Edexcel specification and advised on the provision of Assessment questions.

The authors and publishers are grateful to Edexcel for kind permission to reproduce past examination papers.

Photographs

A1 PIX: 28.2 Superbild; Corbis: A1, page 1 Colin Garratt, page 37 Charles E Rotkin, 18.1 Eye Ubiquitous/Robert & Linda Mostyn, 18.2 Charles Rear, 26.2 TempSport/Jerome Prevost, 28.5 US Naval Observatory, S9 Paul A Souders, M10 Roger Ressmeyer, NP9 David Lees; Getty Images: cover Benelux Press; Martyn Chillmaid: 1.1, 12.3, 28.1, 28.3; NASA: A5; Nelson Thornes: 17.8, S37, Andy Ross 1.5, 2.1, 2.4, 3.1, 3.2, 3.3, 3.4, 3.5, 3.6, 7.2, S27, Alan Thomas 2.6, 5.3, 11.3, S13; Peter Gould: S36a, S36b; Robert Aberman: A3, A4; Science Photo Library: 2.7 Charles D Winters, 18.4a Damien Lovegrove, 18.4c Adam Hart-Davis, A2 top, A2 bottom David Parker, A6 NASA, A7 Space Telescope Institute/NASA, A12 John Chumack, A14 Dr Rudolph Schild, A16 Jeff Hester & Paul Scowen/Arizona State University, S12 Dr Erwin Mueller, S13 Andrew Syred, S14 Andrew Syred, S15 Manfred Kage, M1 Beranger/BSIP, M3 CNRI, M9 Scott Camazine, M14 Matt Meadows, S29, NP1; Zooid: 18.4b; Picture research by Zooid Pictures Ltd and johnbailey@axonimages.com

About the authors

Mark Ellse is Principal of Chase Academy in Cannock, Staffordshire, and a former Principal Examiner for Edexcel.

Chris Honeywill is a Reviser and Acting Principal Examiner for Edexcel and former Head of Physics at Farnborough Sixth Form College.

Electricity

From the basic circuitry of the lamp by your bedside to the complex circuitry creating the immense energy to power Eurostar, electricity drives modern life like few other discoveries of the 19th century. Electricity is that invisible method of working. It is how power stations transfer energy into our homes, to help us work, eat, travel and live. Electricity is so convenient, and so easy to control. In this section, we look at the properties of electricity, how to measure them and thus how to predict their effects on electric circuits, transforming so many things in our lives.

An example of 25 kV at 200 A

What happens in an electric circuit?

Lighting a lamp

- Connect a lamp to a cell (Figure 1.1). Observe what happens.
- What will happen if the lamp is connected to the cell for a long time?
- Predict what will happen if you connect a battery of two cells to the lamp (Figure 1.2). Then test your prediction.
- Repeat with three cells.

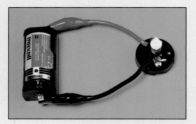

Figure 1.1 Energy is transferred from the cell to the lamp.

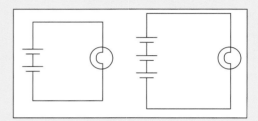

Figure 1.2 Two cells and three cells in series.

Energy from cell to lamp

Figure 1.1 shows a cell connected to a lamp. The lamp filament gets hot, perhaps hot enough to emit light. Energy is transferred from the cell to the lamp; the lamp gains energy from the cell and the cell loses energy to the lamp. Eventually the cell runs down and the lamp goes out.

Like any electrical circuit, Figure 1.1 has a power source (the cell) and a complete circuit. The fact that you need a complete circuit for electrical circuits to work suggests that something is flowing, going into components through one lead and out through the other.

A mechanical analogy

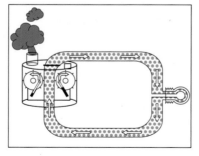

Figure 1.3 A mechanical analogy – the engine pushes the balls around the 'circuit'.

Figure 1.3 shows a similar mechanical situation. The engine pushes balls through a pipe. The balls are like whatever flows round an electrical circuit, and the engine is like whatever does the pushing. The balls flow through the pipe, through the lamp and eventually back to the engine. Where they have to move more quickly through the thin part of the circuit in the lamp they make the pipe hot. Eventually the engine runs out of fuel; it no longer pushes and the flow stops.

Charge carriers

In an electrical circuit, the balls that move are very small and are called **charge carriers**. The 'engine' that pushes them is the chemical reaction in the **cells**. The flow of charge is called a **current**, and it is common to put an arrow on circuits from the part of the supply labelled positive, through the external circuit and back to the part of the cell labelled negative, to show the direction of the current (Figure 1.4).

In most circuits, the charge carriers are electrons, which flow round the circuit from the negative of the cell to the positive, in the opposite direction from the current arrows. But the practical effect is just like pushing positive charge carriers around in the direction shown by the current arrows.

Electrical work

The cell in the circuit applies a force to the charge carriers in the direction in which they move; it *works* on the charge carriers. In turn, the charge carriers work on the lamp filament. **Electrical work** is very similar to mechanical work, but it is invisible. You can detect it only by its effects. When electrical work is done, energy is being transferred.

More cells and more lamps

A group of cells connected together is called a **battery**. Some cells and a battery are shown in Figure 1.5. If you connect a battery of two cells in series to the lamp, the lamp shines more brightly. Both cells push the electrons; the electrons move faster (Figure 1.6). The bigger current makes the lamp brighter.

But if you connect a single cell to two lamps as in Figure 1.7, then the electrons will slow down. There is the same push, but both lamps resist the movement of the electrons.

Direct current (d.c.) and alternating current (a.c.)

In the circuits mentioned so far, the cells push the electrons in one direction only and the electrons travel in this direction. This is **direct current**.

An alternating current power supply pushes the electrons first one way and then the other. The electrons in the circuit move backwards and forwards. The power supply still supplies energy but without the electrons moving steadily in any one direction. The electrons move equally in both directions; they take part in transferring energy from the supply to the load, but they do not themselves go from the supply to the load.

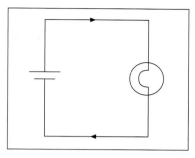

Figure 1.4   Arrows indicate the direction of the current.

Figure 1.5   Alkaline, Leclanché and rechargeable nickel–cadmium cells and 9 V zinc–carbon battery.

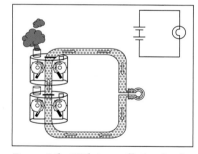

Figure 1.6   With two cells (engines), the electrons (balls) move faster.

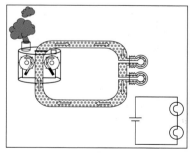

Figure 1.7   Both lamps resist the current, so the flow is less.

2 Charge and current

Polythene strip

- Rub a polythene strip with a duster, and then balance it on an upturned watch glass (Figure 2.1).
- Rub another polythene strip and hold the rubbed end near the rubbed end of the strip on the watch glass. What do you notice?
- Repeat with two acetate strips; then with one acetate strip and one polythene strip.
- Rub the strips again and scrape them on the coulombmeter plate and note the readings.

Figure 2.1   Investigating charge.

Charge

Atoms are mainly protons, neutrons and electrons. Protons and electrons both have **charge** – the property that gives rise to electrical forces. The charge on the electron is called negative, and that on the proton is called positive. Most things, most of the time, have equal numbers of protons and electrons. The charges cancel out and so you do not notice electrical effects. The objects are uncharged or **neutral**. The neutron is neutral.

Electrons are on the outsides of atoms, so they can be moved around. Generally, when you observe electrical effects, it is because electrons have moved around.

Unequal charges

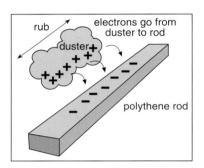

Figure 2.2   Charging a polythene rod.

When you rub a neutral polythene rod with a duster, you transfer electrons from the duster to the rod (Figure 2.2), giving the polythene a surplus of electrons and making it negative. The rod will repel another rubbed polythene rod, because *like charges repel*.

When you rub an acetate rod, electrons go from the rod to the duster (Figure 2.3). The acetate is short of electrons, and therefore positive. An acetate rod will attract a polythene rod because *unlike charges attract*.

Measuring charge

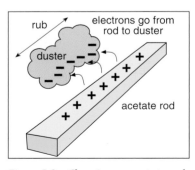

Figure 2.3   Charging an acetate rod.

Since electrons and protons have the same size of charge, you could measure charge in 'electrons worth'. But the charge on an electron is much too small for everyday use as a unit. So the **coulomb** is used. The charge on one electron is 1.6×10^{-19} C. So one coulomb (1 C) is the charge carried by about 6.25×10^{18} electrons. Coulombmeters measure charge and show whether it is positive or negative. They usually measure in nanocoulombs (1 nC = 10^{-9} C), which is the charge carried by 6 250 000 000 electrons. A charged polythene rod may have a charge of hundreds of nanocoulombs, so you can see that vast numbers of electrons move around when you charge a plastic rod.

Discharging a coulombmeter

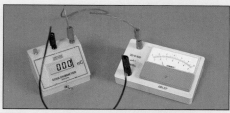

Figure 2.4   Discharging a coulombmeter.

- A coulombmeter stores the charge it measures.
- Charge a coulombmeter with a polythene rod to at least −1000 nC.
- Then discharge it by connecting a microammeter to it as shown.
- Observe the microammeter as the coulombmeter discharges (Figure 2.4).

Moving charge

While the coulombmeter discharges through the microammeter, the extra electrons, which are transferred to the coulombmeter plate while you charge it, run to the other terminal through the microammeter. The microammeter shows a current. This shows that while charge moves you get a current.

Charging a coulombmeter with a known current

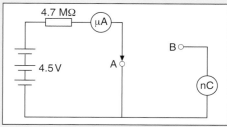

Figure 2.5   Charging a coulombmeter.

- Set up the circuit shown in Figure 2.5.
- Check that the ammeter reads a current of about 1 μA when it is connected to A.
- Zero the coulombmeter and then connect the ammeter to B. Watch what happens.
- Zero the coulombmeter again and measure the charge that flows when a current of 1 μA flows for 1 s.

Calculating charge

The **current** is the rate of flow of charge, that is, the quantity of charge that flows per second. Current is measured in amperes. One ampere (1 A) is equal to one coulomb per second (1 C s^{-1}). When a charge of 1 C flows past a point in 1 s, the current is 1 coulomb per second, that is 1 A. When a charge of 1 μC flows in 1 s, the current is 1 μA. We can write

current = rate of flow of charge

$$I = \frac{\Delta Q}{\Delta t}$$

where I is the current and ΔQ is the charge that flows in a time Δt.

Charge is a derived quantity. It is defined from the base quantities of current and time by the equation $\Delta Q = I\Delta t$.

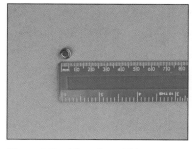

Figure 2.6   A hearing-aid battery will supply 10 μA continuously for 6 months.

Charge and batteries

An ordinary D-size battery can supply 0.3 A for 4 h. This means its capacity is 0.3 A × 4 h = 1.2 A h. It will supply a current of 1.2 A for 1 h, or 0.12 A for 10 h, etc. You can calculate the charge that moves during the lifetime of the battery from these figures. You know that

$$I = \frac{\Delta Q}{\Delta t} \text{ so } \Delta Q = I \Delta t = 0.3 \text{ A} \times (4 \times 3600) \text{ s} = 4320 \text{ C}$$

Two further examples of battery capacity are shown in Figures 2.6 and 2.7. Calculate the charge that moves in each case.

Figure 2.7   A car battery with a capacity of 24 A h.

Current in series circuits

Setting up circuits

Learn the good habit of laying out your circuits neatly and carefully, even with simple circuits. It makes understanding them and finding faults so much easier.

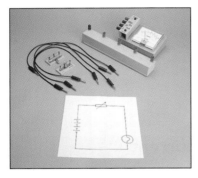

Figure 3.1 First put a copy of the circuit diagram directly in front of you, so that you can compare the circuit diagram with the component layout. If you are stuck, make the copy big and put the components on top of the diagram.

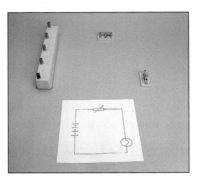

Figure 3.2 Position the components in exactly the same way as they are shown in the circuit diagram.

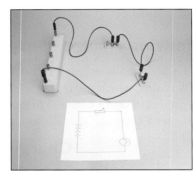

Figure 3.3 Finally, connect the components using leads of the right length to keep the circuit looking just like the circuit diagram.

Using ammeters

You use an ammeter to find the current flowing through a particular point in a circuit.

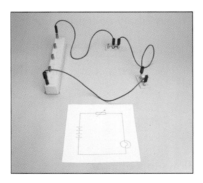

Figure 3.4 First set up the circuit and decide where you wish to measure the current. Then break the circuit at the required point.

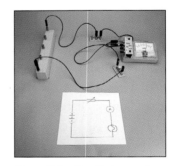

Figure 3.5 Finally insert the ammeter. You should need only a single extra lead. You can then read the meter.

The ammeter is connected *in series with* the current that it is measuring, so the current goes through the ammeter and then continues through the rest of the circuit.

The ammeter deflects in the correct direction if its red terminal is connected nearest to the positive terminal of the power supply. But if the reading is negative, just reverse the connections.

Reading meter scales

Take care when you read meter scales because the numbers on them may not correspond exactly to the values measured.

The meter in Figure 3.6 is measuring the current through the lamp. It uses a 100 mA adapter, called a **shunt**, which allows it to measure up to 100 mA maximum. The shunt is 100 mA f.s.d., which means 100 mA full-scale deflection. This means that when the meter is at full-scale deflection (at its maximum positive reading), the current through the instrument is 100 mA.

There are two scales on the meter. In this case, the top one is the easiest to use, since 10 on the top scale corresponds to 100 mA. So calculate the current that is flowing through the meter by multiplying the top scale reading by 10 mA. The current in this case is 65 mA.

Figure 3.6   An ammeter fitted with a shunt.

With a 500 mA shunt, use the bottom scale and multiply its reading by 100 mA.

Measuring the current in a series circuit

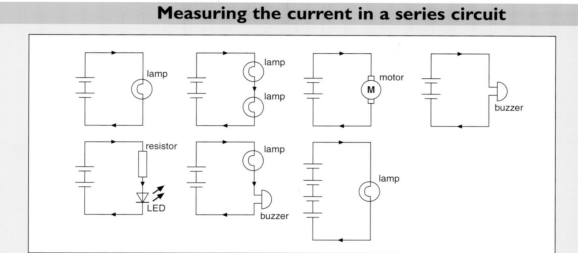

Figure 3.7   Series circuits.

- Set up the circuits in Figure 3.7 and use an ammeter to measure the current through every accessible wire in the circuit.
- When you have done one or two measurements on each circuit, predict what your readings will be before taking the remaining measurements.

What happens in a series circuit?

The circuits in Figure 3.7 are all examples of **series** circuits. The current passes through one component, then through the next, and then through the next, etc. When components are in series, the current through each is the same. The number of electrons that go into a component in each second is the same as the number that come out the other end. Charge and current are not used up by the component: what goes in comes out.

If you think back to the engine diagrams in Chapter 1, this might help you understand what is going on. The number of balls per second going into any component is equal to the number coming out per second.

Kirchhoff's first law

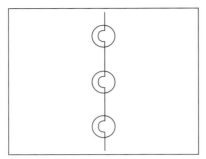

Figure 4.1   Components connected in series.

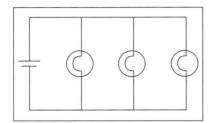

Figure 4.2   Components connected in parallel.

Series and parallel

So far, you have looked at current flowing in a series circuit. But components can be connected in parallel, as well as in series–parallel combinations. Figures 4.1 to 4.3 show all these possibilities.

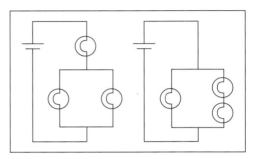

Figure 4.3   Series–parallel arrangements.

Measuring current in parallel circuits

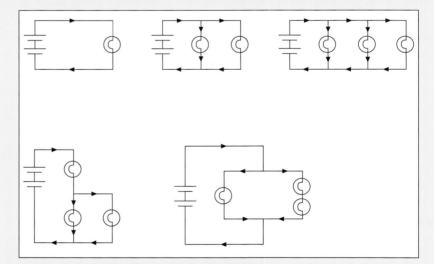

Figure 4.4   Measuring current in parallel circuits.

- Set up the circuits in Figure 4.4 and use an ammeter to measure the current through every accessible wire.
- When you have done one or two measurements on each circuit, predict what the rest of your readings will be before you take the measurements.

Currents in parallel circuits

Figure 4.5 is a **parallel** circuit. The current I_T from the cell splits at the junction. Part of it, I_1, goes through the lamp on the left; the rest, I_2, goes through the lamp on the right. The sum of these two currents I_1 and I_2 is I_T. If the lamps are identical then the two currents will be identical. But components which are in parallel are often different, so the current through them will be different too.

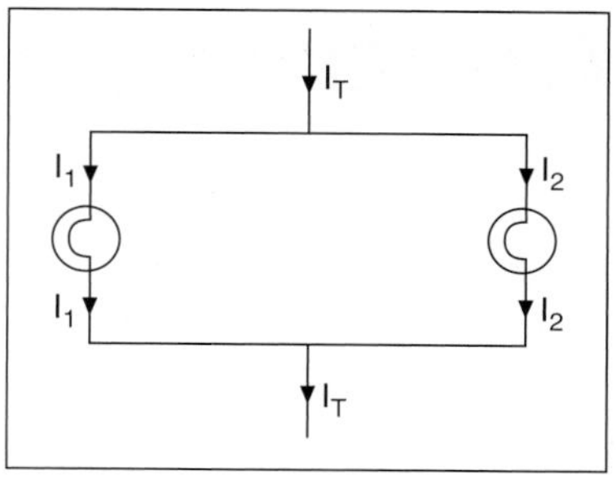

The mechanical circuit in Figure 4.6 gives an idea of what is going on. Some of the balls can take route 1, others take route 2. At point P, the number of balls arriving via route 1 and route 2 is equal to the number leaving by route 3.

Kirchhoff's first law

If you examine a circuit in which a steady current is flowing you find that, at any junction in a circuit, the amount of charge entering is equal to the amount of charge that leaves. Similarly, the rate at which charge flows in to any point is equal to the rate at which charge flows out of the point. The current entering a point is equal to the current leaving that point. This is called **Kirchhoff's first law**:

> **The sum of the currents entering a point is equal to the sum of the currents leaving that point.**

Kirchhoff's first law is a consequence of the fact that charge is conserved. It can be regarded as a law of conservation of charge. It states that no charge is lost in a circuit or at any junction in a circuit.

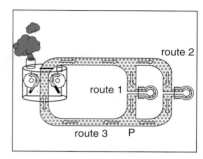

Figure 4.5   Current in a parallel circuit, $I_T = I_1 + I_2$

Figure 4.6   The flow leaving by route 3 is equal to the sum of the flows arriving by routes 1 and 2.

Controlling current

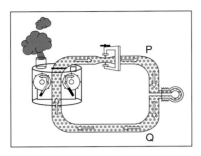

Figure 5.1 *If the pipe is squashed, the current is reduced.*

Reducing the flow

Think about an obstruction in a mechanical circuit (Figure 5.1). What happens to the rate of flow of balls at point P in the circuit when the clamp squashes the pipe? What happens to the rate of flow at Q?

Wherever the pipe is squashed, the current in the *whole circuit* is reduced. If you squash the pipe at P, it reduces the flow at Q as well. Compare this with an electrical circuit.

Measuring current all the way round a series circuit

- Set up the first circuit (Figure 5.2). Note the brightness of the lamp.
- Then set up the next circuit with a resistor.
- Now use a variable resistor. Adjust it and note the effect.
- Put ammeters in the wires and measure the current all the way round.
- Then try putting the resistor on the other side of the lamp.

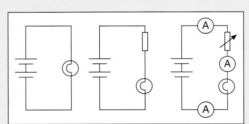

Figure 5.2 *Measuring current in series circuits.*

Controlling current

Resistors oppose the flow of current. Wherever you put them in a circuit, they reduce the current through every component they are in series with. With a large series resistance, the current everywhere is small. If you reduce the series resistance, the current everywhere is larger.

You can put extra resistance into an electrical circuit simply by making part of the wiring thinner. Or you can include a much longer wire. You can also add extra resistance by putting in a piece of material through which electrons find it hard to move, or in which there are very few charge carriers that can move.

Figure 5.3 *A thermistor (left) and a light-dependent resistor (right).*

Electrical sensors

An electrical sensor feeds information into a circuit by allowing a physical quantity outside the circuit to control current flow. Many electrical sensors make use of a changing resistance. One type of light sensor, a **light-dependent resistor** (LDR), changes resistance with the level of illumination. A **thermistor** changes resistance with temperature. Both are shown in Figure 5.3.

Thermistor and LDR

- Use a thermistor and a light-emitting diode to make a crude thermometer using the circuit shown in Figure 5.4.
- Then use a light-dependent resistor in place of the thermistor to make a crude light meter.
- Modify the circuits with a buzzer to make a temperature alarm or a light alarm that will switch a buzzer on if the temperature gets high or if the light gets bright.
- Now try making a circuit that will start a motor when the LDR is illuminated.

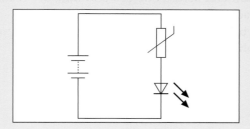

Figure 5.4   A crude thermometer.

Uses of parallel circuits

When power supplies are connected to components in parallel, the current through each branch of the parallel circuit depends mostly on the resistance of the branch itself. Provided that the supply is powerful enough to supply current to all the components that are in parallel, the current through one branch does not affect the current through the others. Car wiring (Figure 5.5), house wiring (Figure 5.6), the wiring of different modules in a piece of electronic equipment, and any other wiring where each part needs to be independent of the other part, all use parallel wiring.

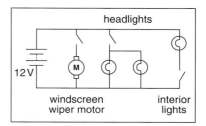

Figure 5.5   Car wiring uses parallel circuits.

Controlling a large current with a small current

An LDR will not pass enough current to run a motor. If you want to make a light-controlled motor, you need a device that will enable a sensor like an LDR, which can control only a small current, to control a larger current. The reed relay (Figure 5.7) uses an electromagnet to control a switch. When a current flows through the electromagnet coil, the switch contacts are magnetised and pull themselves together. The current needed to pull the contacts together is much less than the current that can flow through the contacts. The reed relay can thus control a large current with a small current.

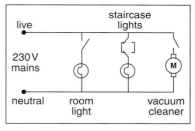

Figure 5.6   House wiring also uses parallel circuits.

The controlling current and the controlled current flow in two loops that have some parts in common and some separate. Where they separate, the components through which they each pass are in parallel.

The transistor

A transistor can also control a large current with a small current. In some ways it is an electronic relay. Figure 5.8 shows how a transistor can be used to help an LDR control a motor.

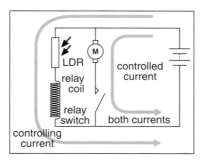

Figure 5.7   Reed relay control (optional).

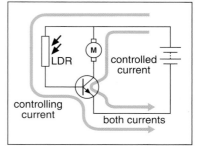

Figure 5.8   Transistor control (optional).

Voltage

Cells and voltage

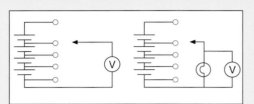

- Set up the circuits shown in Figure 6.1.
- Connect the voltmeter across one cell and note the reading.
- Then measure across two, three and four cells.
- Now observe what happens when you connect a lamp to increasing numbers of cells.

Figure 6.1   What is the effect of the number of cells?

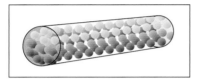

Figure 6.2   With no forces, the balls remain stationary.

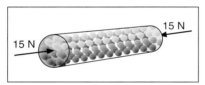

Figure 6.3   With equal forces, the balls also remain stationary.

Figure 6.4   When the forces on the balls are unequal, the balls accelerate.

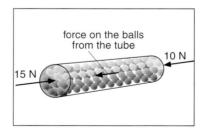

Figure 6.5   When the resistance from the tube equals the external force difference, the balls go at constant speed.

Pushing harder

When you connect cells together in series, the voltmeter indicates a larger voltage. When you increase the number of cells in series to a lamp, the lamp glows brighter, showing that the current is greater. You know that if the current increases then the charge is flowing faster. If the charge is flowing faster through the same resistance, it is being pushed harder. The higher voltage indicates that the charge is being pushed harder.

Creating a flow

Think about a pipe full of balls (Figure 6.2). With no force acting on them, the balls would not accelerate. If they were stationary, they would not start moving.

On the other hand, if there were equal forces at both ends of the pipe (Figure 6.3), the net force would be zero, and the balls would still not accelerate. If stationary, they would still not start to move.

The balls start moving when the force pushing the balls in one direction is greater than the force pushing them in the other direction (Figure 6.4). It is the force difference applied across the tube that starts the balls going.

But there is friction inside the tube, which resists the flow of balls. The balls reach a steady speed when the force difference across the tube is equal to the resistance caused by friction within the tube (Figure 6.5).

The same situation arises with electrons in a wire. When a steady current flows, the average drift speed of the charge carriers is constant. This means that the average resultant force on the carriers is zero. The power supply pushes the electrons in the direction that they are going, and the circuit resistances hinder the flow. So the resultant force on the electrons is zero.

Voltage difference

In a mechanical circuit, *force difference* drives the flow. In electrical circuits, *voltage difference* drives current through a component. If the voltage across a component increases, it pushes the charge carriers harder. They will move faster and the current will increase.

Another name for voltage is potential; it is common to talk about the potential difference (p.d.) across a component. Sometimes this is referred to as the voltage across a component. You connect a voltmeter *across* a component to measure the voltage difference between its ends.

If the voltages at the ends of a component are the same, there is no voltage across the component. So no current will flow. This is like connecting both ends of a component to the same terminal of a battery (Figure 6.6).

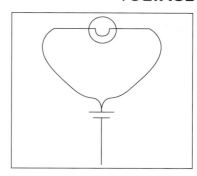

Figure 6.6   If both leads from the lamp are connected to the same terminal, it does not light.

Measuring voltage

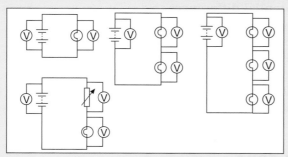

Figure 6.7   Measuring voltage in series circuits.

- Measure the voltages across the components in the circuits shown in Figure 6.7.
- When you have taken one or two measurements on each circuit, predict what the remaining measurements will be before taking them.
- Label your diagrams with the voltages across each component.

Pushing and resisting

If, as you go round a circuit, you keep the terminals of your voltmeter the same way round, you find that for some components the reading is positive; for the rest, the reading is negative.

As you move the voltmeter clockwise round the circuit of Figure 6.8, keeping its negative terminal anticlockwise of the positive terminal, the meter goes positive for those components which are helping charge move (in this case the cells) and negative for those which are resisting. If you go right round any series circuit, the sum of the voltages across the components pushing is equal to the sum of the voltages across the components resisting.

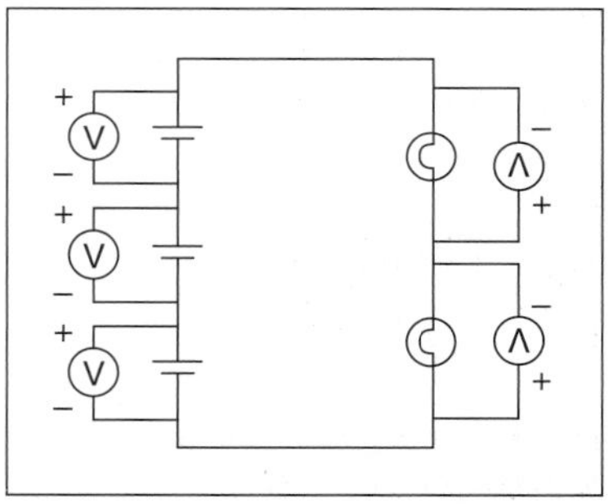

Electrical and water currents

The flow of balls through a pipe is something like the flow of a current of water through a pipe. Indeed the analogy is very close if you think of water as made up of many ball-like atoms. It is *pressure difference* that drives water flow, and this is a better analogy for voltage difference than the model with force difference. Pressure, like voltage, is a scalar quantity, whereas force is a vector. Voltage or pressure differences drive electrical or water currents. Electrical or pipe resistances oppose the flow. In both situations, the rate of flow is the current.

Figure 6.8   Keeping the voltmeter the same way round shows which components are helping and which are hindering.

7 | Electrical power and energy calculations

Electromotive forces – energy givers

Some components in an electrical circuit push the charge carriers in the direction the carriers move. They are working on the charge and so give energy to the circuit. Components like cells and generators do work on the charge. Voltages across these components are called **electromotive forces** (e.m.f.s), because they apply forces that make the charge move.

Potential differences – energy takers

The other components in the circuit, the wires, the lamps, the resistors, etc, apply forces in the opposite direction to the direction the charge is moving. The charge does work on them, transferring energy to them. The voltages across them are called **potential differences** (p.d.s). As you would expect, the total amount of energy given to a circuit by the e.m.f. is equal to the total amount of energy taken by the p.d.s. Around a loop in a series circuit, the e.m.f.s = the p.d.s (Figure 7.1). You might like to reread the section 'Pushing and resisting' in Chapter 6 and compare it with this statement. (The term 'potential difference' is mostly used for energy takers, but sometimes used for energy givers as well. It does, however, help to keep the ideas separate if you use the different terms.)

> Some teachers think that it is confusing to know that emf involves the word 'force'. See pages 35–6 for the proper definition of emf.

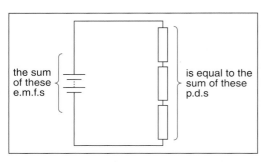

Figure 7.1 The e.m.f.s = the p.d.s.

the sum of these e.m.f.s

is equal to the sum of these p.d.s

Calculating work done

Voltage can be used to calculate the work done pushing the charge carriers round a circuit or through a component. The **voltage** between two points is the work done per coulomb travelling between the two points. That is

$$\text{voltage} = \frac{\text{work}}{\text{charge}}$$

$$V = \frac{W}{Q}$$

So the unit of voltage, the volt, is the same as the units of work/charge, i.e., joule/coulomb:

$$1\,V = 1\,J\,C^{-1}$$

If the voltage across the cell in Figure 7.2 is 1.5 V, the cell gives 1.5 joules per coulomb that travels between the terminals. There is, of course, a voltage of 1.5 V across the lamp as well. So 1.5 J of work is done on the lamp every time a coulomb goes through the lamp.

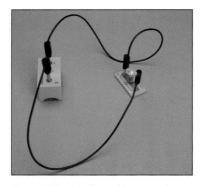

Figure 7.2 A cell working on a lamp.

If a 230 V power supply is connected to a motor, then the work done when 8 coulombs flow can be calculated by:

$$\text{work} = \text{voltage} \times \text{charge} = 230\,J\,C^{-1} \times 8\,C = 1840\,J$$

So 1840 joules of energy is transferred from the power supply to the motor when 8 coulombs flow.

Measuring work and power

- Connect a power supply to a lamp. Measure the voltage across the lamp and the current through the lamp.
- Calculate how much charge passes through the lamp in one minute. Then calculate the work done in that time.
- Calculate the charge that flows in one second and the work done in a second.

Calculating power

$$\text{voltage} = \frac{\text{work}}{\text{charge}}$$

$$\therefore \text{work} = \text{voltage} \times \text{charge}$$

Power is the work done per second,
so

$$\text{power} = \frac{\text{work}}{\text{time}} = \frac{\text{voltage} \times \text{charge}}{\text{time}} = \text{voltage} \times \frac{\text{charge}}{\text{time}}$$

$$\therefore \text{power} = \text{voltage} \times \text{current}$$

$$P = VI$$

You can use this equation to define the voltage between two points as the power transferred to the circuit between those points per amp.

The unit of power is, of course, the joule per second or watt.

As   power = voltage × current
you can see that

$$\frac{\text{joule}}{\text{second}} = \frac{\text{joule}}{\text{coulomb}} \times \frac{\text{coulomb}}{\text{second}}$$

Voltage across components in series

When components are in series (Figure 7.3), the total voltage across all the components is equal to the sum of the voltages across each individual component.

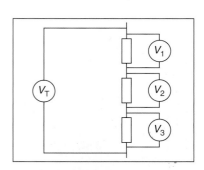

Figure 7.3   Voltage across components in series,
$V_T = V_1 + V_2 + V_3.$

Electrical height

Measuring voltage in parallel circuits

- Set up the circuits in Figure 8.1 and measure the voltages across each component.
- Then try other circuits.
- What rules can you find for the voltages across components that are in parallel?

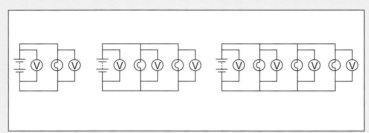

Figure 8.1   Measuring voltage in parallel circuits.

Voltage across components in parallel

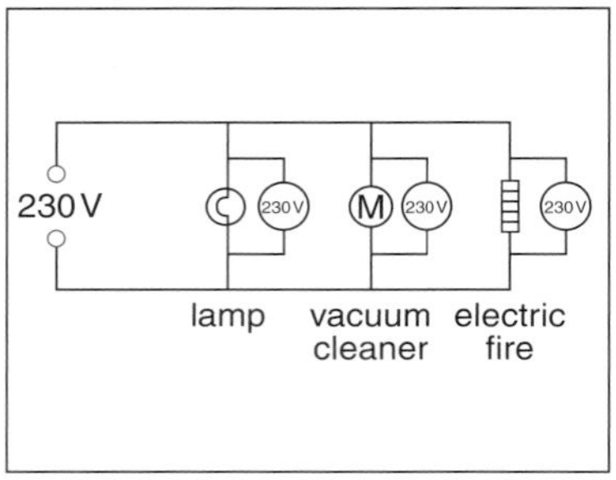

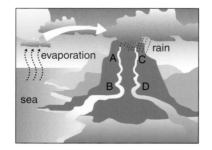

Figure 8.2   Components connected to the mains supply are in parallel. They have the same voltage across them.

When components are in parallel, the voltage across each component is the same. In Chapter 5 you learned that the currents in a parallel circuit can be more or less independent of each other, which is why components are connected in parallel when connected to a car battery or the mains supply (Figure 8.2). Now you can see that components connected in parallel have the same voltage across them. A 230 V lamp can be connected in parallel with a 230 V vacuum cleaner and a 230 V electric fire, all to a 230 V supply, and they all have the same supply voltage.

Flowing streams

Sometimes it is useful to think of an electric current as being rather like a water current.

Imagine a mountain with two streams flowing down it (Figure 8.3). The streams flow because the mountain is sloping. The water flows from high parts to lower parts.

Is it height that causes a stream to flow? No, it is not. Water high up on mountains is often in still pools. Even though it is high, it is not flowing. On the other hand you find flowing streams in low valleys. Water does not need to be high in order to flow.

Figure 8.3   A water circuit.

What you need to make water flow is a height difference and a suitable pathway. Water flows from one place to another if the first place is high and the second place is low. On the two streams, points A, B, C and D are marked. A and C are at the same height; B and D are at the same height. If you dug a channel from A to C (Figure 8.4) there would be no height difference and no flow. The same would happen if you dug a channel from B to D. But if you dug a channel from A to D (Figure 8.5) then there would be a height difference and the water would flow. The rate of flow (the current) would depend on the height difference and the size of the channel. A short fat channel would have a low resistance to water flow and the current would be relatively high. The current in a long thin channel would be relatively small.

In the water circuit, rain provides the water for the streams. As the streams flow into the valleys, the sun causes evaporation, which supplies the clouds. This completes the water circuit. In the steady state, the amount of water flowing down the mountain is equal to the amount being taken up by evaporation.

Electrical height

In the water cycle, the sun provides the power source to pump the water around and the flow is a water current. In an electrical circuit, a battery or a generator provides the power source to pump the charge around. The flow of charge is a current. In both circuits, the current is larger if the paths are short and fat.

Look at the two 'electrical streams' in Figure 8.6. The battery pushes charge 'uphill' to the top of the circuit and the charge flows 'downhill' through the two chains of resistors. If all the resistors are identical, you can see that point A is at the same electrical height as point C. There is no electrical height difference between points A and C. It does not matter what wires, resistors or meters you connect between points A and C, no current will flow between these two points. Similarly, there is no electrical height difference between points B and D, and no current will flow in a wire that connects them.

But there *is* an electrical height difference between points A and D; a current will flow in any wire you connect between them. You know that it is voltage difference that drives a current. Voltage (or potential) is the electrical equivalent of height.

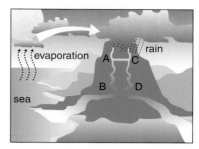

Figure 8.4   There is no flow through this channel from A to C, because there is no height difference.

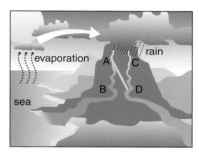

Figure 8.5   The height difference between A and D causes the flow through the channel.

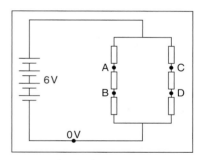

Figure 8.6   The battery pushes charge through the electrical streams AB and CD.

Kirchhoff's second law

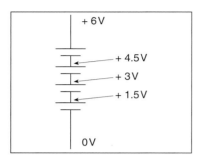

Figure 9.1   Voltages at different points in a battery.

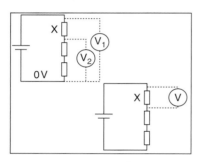

Figure 9.2   Two ways of measuring the voltage across a component X: (a) either measure the voltage at each end of X and subtract them, $V_X = V_1 - V_2$; or (b) measure the voltage across X directly, $V_X = V$.

Voltage at a point

You can mark heights on a map to show how much higher, or lower, a point is relative to some reference level (usually sea level). Similarly, if you want to mark voltages on a circuit, you need to choose some point as a zero of voltage. In experiments with electrostatics you may use the earth on which you are standing as the zero of potential. Electrical engineers commonly choose a reference point for all their voltage measurements which they label 0 V. This point is usually at the bottom of a circuit, but sometimes it is in the middle. The **voltage at a point** in the circuit is the voltage difference between zero and that point. Figure 9.1 shows a battery with the voltages at different points labelled.

If you look back to Figure 8.6, you see that the bottom line is labelled 0 V. That is the zero of voltage for that circuit. The battery is a 6 V battery. That means that the top line of the circuit has a voltage of +6 V. If the resistors are all identical, you can calculate that the voltages at points A and C are +4 V and the voltages at points B and D are +2 V.

Voltage across a component

The **voltage across a component** is simply the difference in voltage between the two ends. You can use a voltmeter to measure the voltage at each end relative to 0 V and then subtract the readings, or you can simply connect a voltmeter across the two points to measure the voltage difference directly (Figure 9.2).

If you look back again to Figure 8.6, you can work out that the voltage difference between A and B (the voltage across the middle resistor) is 2 V. Similarly, the voltage across the bottom left or bottom right resistor is 2 V.

Measuring voltages at different points

- For each circuit in Figure 9.3, connect the 0 V terminal of a digital voltmeter to the part of the circuit marked 0 V.
- Use the other lead to measure the voltage at point A.
- Then predict what the voltages might be at points B to E, before measuring them.

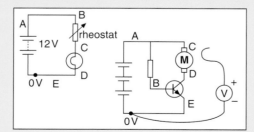

Figure 9.3   Circuits for measurement of voltage at different positions.

Voltage–position graph

Figure 9.4 shows a series circuit with a graph of potential plotted against position for that circuit. Notice how the voltage increases through the e.m.f. and decreases through the p.d.s. Notice also the small voltages across the connecting wires that drive the current through them.

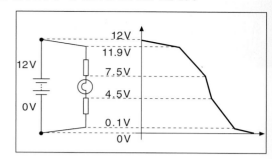

Figure 9.4   A series circuit and its voltage–position graph.

Kirchhoff's second law

Think what happens if you take a walk up a hill and back down again, a closed loop. When you arrive back at your starting point, you are back at the same height you were at in the beginning. For the whole loop, the amount of height gained is equal to the amount of height lost.

Kirchhoff's second law states the equivalent for an electrical circuit. It states that, around a closed loop in a circuit, the gain in voltage is equal to the loss in voltage. In other words, you arrive back at the same electrical height that you started from. The gains in voltage are caused by the e.m.f.s, the drops are caused by the p.d.s. **Kirchhoff's second law** states that:

> **Around any closed loop, the sum of the e.m.f.s is equal to the sum of the p.d.s.**

Kirchhoffs second law is a statement about voltage, and since voltage is a measure of the work done, or energy transferred, per unit charge, this means that Kirchhoffs second law is also a statement about energy. It states that the total amount of energy gained by a coulomb going round a complete circuit is equal to the total amount of energy lost. In this way you can regard Kirchhoffs second law as one version of the law of conservation of energy.

Figure 9.5 shows two circuit diagrams showing typical voltages at various points. Look at the diagrams. You may not understand every circuit symbol, but do the voltages make sense? Work out which way currents would flow if wires were connected between different points in the circuit.

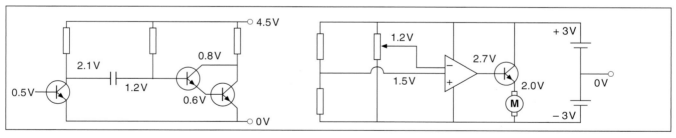

Figure 9.5   Two circuits with typical voltages marked.

10 Resistance

What is resistance?

All components need a voltage to push current through them. When the resistance is high you need a large voltage for a given current. When the resistance is low you need a small voltage. The **resistance** indicates the voltage you need for each amp of current:

$$\text{resistance} = \frac{\text{voltage}}{\text{current}}$$

$$R = \frac{V}{I}$$

The unit of resistance is the volt per amp, which is called the ohm (Ω).

Measuring resistance

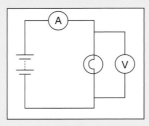

Figure 10.1 Finding the resistance of a component by measuring the voltage across it and the current through it.

- Use a voltmeter and ammeter to measure the resistances of a range of components (Figure 10.1).
- Then connect two or more of them in series and investigate how the total resistance depends on the individual resistances.
- Then connect your components in parallel pairs and investigate how the total resistance depends on the individual resistances.

Resistors in series

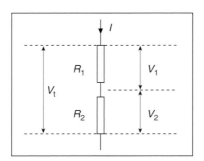

Figure 10.2 Resistors in series.

The total resistance of a number of components in series is simply the sum of the individual resistances.

Resistances R_1 and R_2 are connected in series with a current I flowing through them (Figure 10.2). The voltage across the whole, V_t, is the sum of the individual voltages across each resistor:

$$V_t = V_1 + V_2$$

The equivalent resistance, R_t, is defined by

$$V_t = IR_t$$

But $V_1 = IR_1$ and $V_2 = IR_2$. Therefore

$$IR_t = IR_1 + IR_2$$

$$R_t = R_1 + R_2$$

Resistors in parallel

Each extra resistor in parallel provides an additional path for current to go through, and so allows more current for a given voltage. The resistance of a number of resistors in parallel is *less* than the smallest of the individual resistances.

The voltage across the resistors in Figure 10.3 is V. The total current I_t flowing into and out of the parallel combination is the sum of the currents I_1 and I_2 through the individual resistors:

$$I_t = I_1 + I_2$$

The equivalent resistance, R_t, is defined by

$$R_t = \frac{V}{I_t}$$

Therefore $I_t = \dfrac{V}{R_t}$. Similarly $I_1 = \dfrac{V}{R_1}$ and $I_2 = \dfrac{V}{R_2}$. Since $I_t = I_1 + I_2$,

$$\frac{V}{R_t} = \frac{V}{R_1} + \frac{V}{R_2}$$

$$\frac{1}{R_t} = \frac{1}{R_1} + \frac{1}{R_2}$$

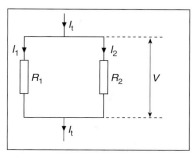

Figure 10.3   Resistors in parallel.

For a resistance of 220 Ω in parallel with a resistance of 470 Ω,

$$\frac{1}{R_t} = \frac{1}{R_1} + \frac{1}{R_2}$$

$$\frac{1}{R_t} = \frac{1}{220\ \Omega} + \frac{1}{470\ \Omega}$$

$$\frac{1}{R_t} = 6.67 \times 10^{-3}\ \Omega^{-1}$$

$$R_t = 150\ \Omega$$

Calculating power from current through resistance

When a current flows through a resistor, work is done on that resistor. You can calculate the power, the rate of working, directly from the current and resistance.

When a resistor is connected to a voltage V, power $= VI$
But the voltage across the resistor, $V = IR$. So

$$\text{power} = (IR) \times I = I^2 R$$

If a resistance of 6.8 kΩ has a current of 2.2 mA flowing through it,

$$\text{power} = I^2 R = (2.2 \times 10^{-3}\ \text{A})^2 \times 6.8 \times 10^3\ \Omega = 0.033\ \text{W} = 33\ \text{mW}$$

When a current flows through a resistor, we sometimes say that the power is **dissipated**. This means scattered. The internal energy of the resistor has increased, and this random kinetic and potential energy gradually spreads to the surroundings. You can read more about energy dissipation in the next section of this book.

Change of resistance

Different ways of measuring voltage and current

- Set up the circuits in Figures 11.1 and 11.2.
- Use these two different circuits to measure the voltage across, and the current through, the 10 kΩ resistor.
- Take the readings very carefully indeed and compare them.
- Then use a digital ohmmeter to measure the resistance as in Figure 11.3.

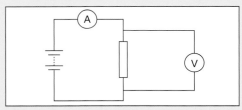

Figure 11.1   Circuit 1 for measuring voltage and current.

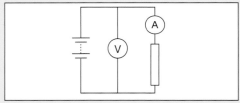

Figure 11.2   Circuit 2 for measuring voltage and current.

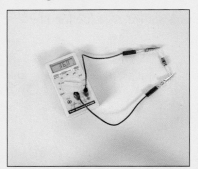

Figure 11.3   You can use a digital ohmmeter to measure resistance directly.

Errors caused by voltmeters and ammeters

The two arrangements of the meters for measuring *V–I* characteristics (Figures 11.1 and 11.2) both introduce small errors in measurement.

As you will read in Chapter 15, even though the resistance of voltmeters is high, they draw a tiny current when you connect them to a voltage. In Figure 11.1, the voltmeter reads correctly, but the ammeter measures the current through the resistor and the voltmeter. So there is a small error since you assume that the ammeter reading is the current through the resistor alone.

Ammeters have a small but significant resistance; when current flows through them, there is a voltage across them. In Figure 11.2, the ammeter reads correctly, but the voltmeter measures the voltage across both resistor and ammeter, not just across the resistor, so there is a small error since you assume that the voltmeter is just measuring the voltage across the resistor.

The first circuit produces significant errors when the current through the voltmeter is significant compared with the current through the resistor; the second produces significant errors when the potential difference across the ammeter is significant compared with the potential difference across the resistor.

Digital ohmmeters (Figure 11.3) measure the resistance directly and have neither error.

Change of resistance

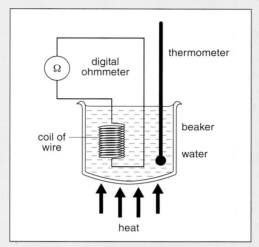

Figure 11.4 *The resistance of a metal wire at constant temperature.*

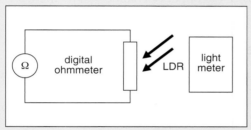

Figure 11.5 *The resistance of an LDR.*

- Set up the apparatus shown in Figure 11.4.
- Measure the resistance of a coil of 10 m of thin insulated copper wire over a range of temperatures.
- Plot a graph of resistance against temperature.

- Measure the resistance of a negative-temperature-coefficient thermistor over a range of temperatures. Plot a graph of resistance against temperature.

- Illuminate a light-dependent resistor with a lamp. Use a light meter to measure the level of illumination and a digital ohmmeter to measure the resistance.
- Change the illumination by moving the lamp closer and further away. Measure the resistance of a light-dependent resistor for a range of values of illumination (Figure 11.5). Plot a graph of resistance against light intensity measured with a light meter.

Change of resistance with temperature

The resistance of a metal wire increases as its temperature rises while the resistance of a negative-temperature-coefficient thermistor decreases.

Change of resistance with illumination

The resistance of a light-dependent resistor decreases as the light intensity falling on it increases.

You will read in Chapter 13 about how these changes in resistance occur.

12 How fast does charge move?

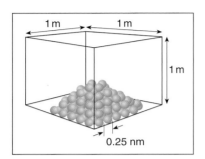

Figure 12.1 A cubical array of copper atoms.

Free charge in a conductor

Most of the electrons in metallic conductors are fixed to their atoms, but for each atom, one or two electrons are free to move and carry charge. If you calculate how many atoms there are in a cubic metre, you can estimate the number of free electrons per cubic metre.

The atoms in copper have a diameter of about 0.25 nm. Assume that they are stacked together cubically, as shown in Figure 12.1. There will be 1 m/0.25 nm = 4×10^9 atoms along each edge of a one-metre cube. Therefore there will be $(4 \times 10^9)^3 = 6.4 \times 10^{28}$ atoms in a cubic metre. Assuming one free electron per atom, this gives a figure of about 6.4×10^{28} electrons per cubic metre. This is known as the **charge carrier density** or just as the **carrier density**. It has the symbol n.

The free charge in a metre cube is therefore about $6.4 \times 10^{28} \times 1.6 \times 10^{-19}$ = 1.0×10^{10} coulomb, so in a piece of copper of volume 1 mm³, there are 10 C of free charge.

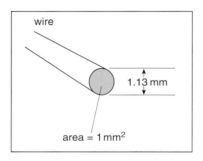

Figure 12.2 The wire has a cross-sectional area of 1 mm².

How fast does charge move?

Electrical effects happen very quickly. A lamp seems to light almost instantly when you connect it to a power supply, even if the leads are very long. It makes it interesting to consider how quickly the charge flows. A typical copper connecting wire (Figure 12.2) has a cross-sectional area of 1 mm². If free electrons in the wire move at 1 mm s⁻¹, then 1 mm³ of electrons pass a point each second. From the paragraph above, you know that this corresponds to a charge of 10 C flowing, and if 10 C flow past a point in a second, the current is 10 A.

A small torch bulb may take a current of 0.2 A (Figure 12.3), which is 1/50th of 10 A. So the charge must be moving at 1/50th of the speed that it would do in a wire carrying 10 A, which is 1/50th mm s⁻¹. How can this slow charge speed be compatible with a lamp lighting nearly as soon as you turn it on?

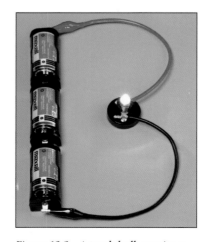

Figure 12.3 A torch bulb carries a current of about 0.2 A.

Why so fast, when the charge moves so slowly?

When you turn a circuit on, electrons throughout the circuit start moving almost straight away. It is rather like pushing balls through a tube. As soon as a ball goes in to one end of a tube another ball comes out of the far end (Figure 12.4). It isn't necessary for the ball to get from one end to the other before the effects are evident at the far end.

Electrical effects are not quite instantaneous. The information that starts the electrons moving travels around the circuit at the speed of light in the form of an electromagnetic wave; so electrical effects travel at the speed of light.

Calculating the speed of charge movement

The wire shown in Figure 12.5 has a charge carrier density n, each carrier having charge q and moving at speed v (called the **drift speed**). The wire has a cross-sectional area A and the current through it is I.

The volume of charge carriers passing a point in 1 s is Av.
So the number of charge carriers passing a point in one second is nAv.
But

current = charge past a point in 1 s = $nAvq$

Therefore

$$I = nAqv$$

You can use this formula to calculate the drift speed of electrons in a copper wire of cross-sectional area 1 mm², carrying a current of 0.2 A. Rearranging it gives

$$v = \frac{I}{nAq}$$

$$= \frac{0.2 \text{ A}}{(6.4 \times 10^{28} \text{ m}^{-3} \times 1 \times 10^{-6} \text{ m}^2 \times 1.6 \times 10^{-19} \text{ C})}$$

$$= 0.02 \text{ mm s}^{-1}$$

This is the same figure as was calculated earlier. This speed is a typical speed for electrons travelling in a conductor. Imagine how slow it is! It is tiny compared with the random motion that the electrons have irrespective of the current that they are carrying. Chapter 13 discusses the motion of charge carriers in more detail.

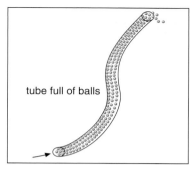

Figure 12.4   As soon as you push a ball into one end, a ball comes out of the other.

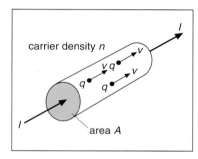

Figure 12.5   A wire carrying a current.

Conduction by coloured ions

- Some chemicals have coloured ions that you can see moving in solution.
- Connect up the apparatus as in Figure 12.6. Wet the filter paper with ammonium solution and put on a single crystal of copper sulphate and a single crystal of potassium permanganate.
- Observe the speed of movement of the ions.
- The copper ion is blue and the permanganate ion is purple. What can you deduce about the charges on the ions?

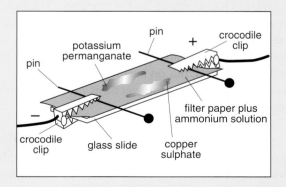

Figure 12.6   You can see coloured manganate and copper ions moving.

Resistivity

What affects the resistance of a wire?

- Use an ohmmeter to measure the resistance of different lengths of a constant thickness of thin nichrome wire.
- Plot a graph to determine the relationship between resistance and length.
- Then measure the resistance of equal lengths of a range of thicknesses. Use a micrometer to measure their diameters and calculate their cross-sectional areas.
- Plot a graph to determine the relationship between resistance and cross-sectional area.
- Repeat with wires made from different metals.

Resistivity

Table 13.1 *The resistivities of various materials*

Material	Resistivity/Ω m^{-1}
metals	
copper	1.7×10^{-8}
iron	10×10^{-8}
semiconductors	
graphite	10^{-5} (very variable)
silicon	10^5
insulators	
paraffin wax	10^{15}
porcelain	10^{20}

The resistance of a wire depends on several factors. A long wire has a larger resistance than a short wire. A fat wire has a lower resistance than a thin wire. Resistance is proportional to length and inversely proportional to cross-sectional area; and it depends on a property of the material called **resistivity**. So

$$\text{resistance} = \text{resistivity} \times \frac{\text{length}}{\text{area}}; \qquad R = \frac{\rho l}{A}$$

Resistivity, ρ, is a property of the material (whereas resistance is a property of a component). Resistivity is a measure of how the material opposes the current through it. Metals have a low resistivity; insulators have a high resistivity. Semiconductors, as their name implies, are somewhere in the middle (Table 13.1).

For example, the resistance of 100 m of copper wire, cross-sectional area 1.5 mm^2, is found by:

$$R = \frac{\rho l}{A} = \frac{1.72 \times 10^{-8}\,\Omega\,\text{m} \times 100\,\text{m}}{1.5 \times 10^{-6}\,\text{m}^2} = 1.15\,\Omega$$

Electrons drifting

The evidence for what goes on inside a conducting material is indirect. Physicists make a model for conduction which fits the evidence. The outer electrons of the atoms in a metal are free from their parent atom, leaving behind an ion vibrating about a fixed position. At normal temperatures, with no current flowing, electrons in a wire hurtle around continuously (Figure 13.1). They keep colliding with the metal ions, but on balance no energy is transferred from electrons to the ions. Since the electrons move randomly, there is no net movement of charge in any direction.

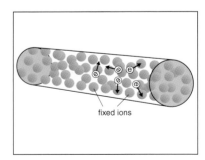

fixed ions

Figure 13.1   Even when no current flows, electrons hurtle about at random within a wire, continually hitting fixed ions.

When a power supply is connected across a wire, it causes electrons to accelerate from negative to positive. The electrons then collide with the fixed ions and move off in random directions and are then accelerated again by the power supply (Figure 13.2). The electrons are continuously gaining energy from the supply and giving it to the ions when they collide. The ions gain energy and the metal gets hotter.

The constant acceleration and collision result in a steady, slow drift along the conductor, superimposed on top of the huge random velocities. This tiny drift speed of a fraction of a millimetre per second is almost unobservable on top of the random velocity of hundreds of metres per second. But it is responsible for all the electrical effects you observe.

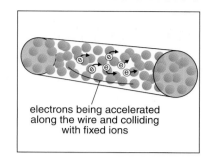

electrons being accelerated along the wire and colliding with fixed ions

Figure 13.2 When a power supply is connected across a wire, the free electrons accelerate along the wire, and hit the fixed ions harder.

Change of carrier speed with temperature

For all materials the fixed ions have larger vibrations at higher temperatures, and increased vibrations impede further the movement of electrons through the metal, tending to reduce the drift speed of the carriers. For pure metals this is the dominant effect, and it means that the resistance of a metal increases with temperature. In other materials this effect is present, though it is not always the most important effect.

Changes in carrier density

In **metals**, the carrier density n is high and does not change with temperature. In **semiconductors**, the carrier density is much smaller but increases strongly with temperature. Therefore, unless some other effect intervenes, the resistivity of a semiconductor decreases with temperature. Thermistors and light-dependent resistors are made of semiconductor materials.

Change of resistance and the equation $I = nAqv$

In metals, currents involve large numbers of charge carriers moving very slowly. When the temperature increases, the drift speed v decreases although the charge-carrier density n is constant. So, although the area A and carrier charge q are constant, the current I in a metallic conductor decreases with temperature because v decreases while n stays the same.

In semiconductors, currents are produced by many fewer carriers moving comparatively quickly. As with metals, the drift speed of the carriers tends to decrease with increasing temperature, but the carrier density increases enormously at higher temperatures. So, while the area A and carrier charge q are constant, the current I in a semiconductor increases with temperature because, although v decreases a little with temperature, n increases enormously. Negative-temperature-coefficient (NTC) thermistors behave like this. Light-dependent resistors also make use of changing n. When they are illuminated, photons in the incident radiation free charge carriers, so they conduct much better and their resistance falls.

For insulators, n is very small indeed at normal temperatures, but increases for all insulators if the temperature is raised sufficiently for the atomic structure to break down into charged particles. So insulators start to conduct if their temperature is raised enough.

The potential divider

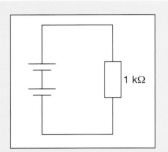

Figure 14.1   Measure the voltage across one 1 kΩ resistor.

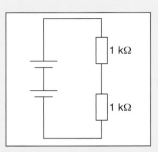

Figure 14.2   Measure the voltages across two 1 kΩ resistors in series.

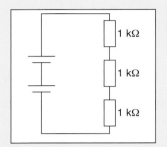

Figure 14.3   Measure the voltages across three 1 kΩ resistors in series.

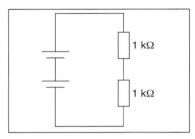

Figure 14.4   If the resistors are identical, then the voltages across each are the same. The voltage across each is half of the whole.

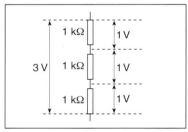

Figure 14.5   With three identical resistors in series, the voltage across each is one-third of the whole.

Chains of resistors

Experiments with a series of identical resistors show that the voltage across each of them is the same and adds up to the voltage across the whole chain (Figures 14.1 – 14.5). With a series of resistors, you can divide a voltage into any fraction.

Flowing downhill

Think back to the height analogy of an electrical circuit. Current is flowing down a resistance chain rather like water flowing down a hillside (Figure 14.6). If the stream flows along a uniform channel down a smooth slope, the midpoint B will be half-way down the hill. The height difference BC is half the height difference AC. In the electrical circuit, the voltage difference BC is half of the voltage difference AC.

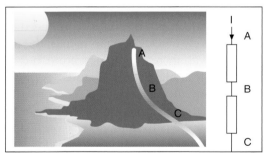

Figure 14.6   Current flows through a chain of resistors like water through a channel.

The voltages across different resistors

- Connect a 1 kΩ and a 2 kΩ resistor in series across a power supply and measure the voltage across each.
- Predict your results before measuring.

Chains of different resistors

If the two resistors in series are different, there are different voltages across them. For instance, if the bottom resistor is twice the resistance of the top resistor (Figure 14.7), it behaves like two resistors connected in series and there is twice as much voltage across it.

Experiments with a range of resistances show that the ratio of the voltages across the resistors is equal to the ratio of the resistances.

In circuit diagrams resistors have standard-sized symbols, but it helps understanding to think of drawing the resistors with length proportional to resistance. In Figure 14.8 the voltage across the top resistance is smaller than the voltage across the bottom one.

Circuits like these are voltage dividers, but they are usually called **potential dividers**. They divide the voltage or p.d. from a source in proportion to their resistances.

Calculating the output of a potential divider

Think of a potential divider (Figure 14.9) as having an input connected to a power supply (V_{in}) and an output (V_{out}). The input voltage to the circuit is the voltage across both resistors. The output voltage is the voltage across the bottom resistor. Provided that no current is drawn from the output, the same current I flows through both resistors.

$$I = \frac{V_{out}}{R_{bottom}} = \frac{V_{in}}{R_{top} + R_{bottom}}$$

$$\therefore \quad V_{out} = V_{in} \frac{R_{bottom}}{R_{top} + R_{bottom}}$$

For example, if the top resistance is 1.2 kΩ and the bottom resistance 720 Ω, then the output, when connected to an input of 12 V, is

$$V_{out} = V_{in} \frac{R_{bottom}}{(R_{top} + R_{bottom})} = 12\,V \times \frac{720\ \Omega}{1200\ \Omega + 720\ \Omega} = 4.5\ v$$

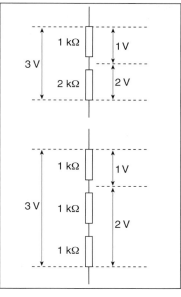

Figure 14.7   The 2 kΩ resistor is like two 1 kΩ resistors in series.

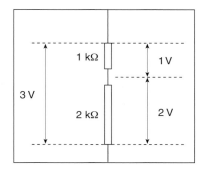

Figure 14.8   Most of the voltage is across the largest resistor.

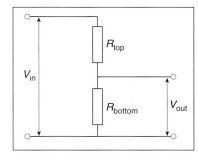

Figure 14.9   The potential divider.

Controlling voltage

Providing a variable voltage

- Look at the circuits shown in Figures 15.1 and 15.2.
- Use your understanding of the potential divider to predict how they will control the voltages across the two lamps.
- Then set up the circuits and test your predictions.

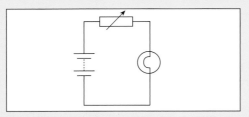

Figure 15.1   Controlling a lamp with a rheostat.

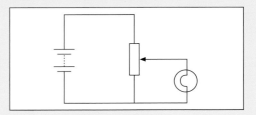

Figure 15.2   Controlling a lamp with a potentiometer.

Rheostats

A variable resistance in series with a component is often called a **rheostat**. It controls the current through the component. A rheostat has a maximum resistance and so some current will still flow through it even at this setting. So it cannot reduce and control the current down to zero.

Potentiometers

A **potentiometer** is a variable potential divider. A sliding contact can connect anywhere from one end to the other of a resistor chain and so can take any fraction of the whole voltage. So it can control the voltage across a component, and therefore the current through it, from maximum down to zero (Figure 15.3).

Although linear (straight) potentiometers are available, most potentiometers are circular (Figure 15.4).

Loading potentiometers

When a resistance is connected to the output of the potential divider, it is connected in parallel with the bottom resistor of the potential divider. The combined resistance at the bottom of the potential divider is less and so this lowers the output voltage of the potential divider. This is called loading the potential divider (Figure 15.5).

Digital voltmeters are electronic voltmeters. A battery inside them supplies the operating current. These voltmeters have high resistance and they draw very little current from the circuit to which they are connected. The load they present to the potential divider is usually negligible and they usually hardly affect the voltage they are measuring.

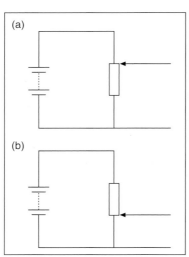

Figure 15.3   The output of a potentiometer can vary from (a) maximum to (b) zero.

Analogue voltmeters, unless they are electronic ones, need to draw enough current from the circuit to which they are connected to move the mechanical pointer. Even though their resistance is high, the small current they draw can significantly change the voltage they measure if you connect them to a potential divider made of high resistances.

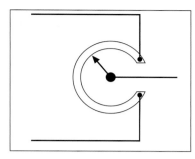

Figure 15.4   Volume controls for radios and amplifiers use circular potentiometers. You rotate a shaft to move the contact.

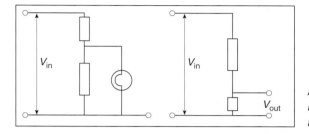

Figure 15.5   The lamp in parallel with the lower resistance reduces the total resistance at the bottom.

Light- and temperature-sensitive potential dividers

- Set up the circuit shown in Figure 15.6
- Use a voltmeter to find out how V_{out} depends on the level of illumination.
- Then exchange the position of the LDR and the resistance and find how the circuit behaves differently.
- Repeat the exercise using a thermistor instead of an LDR and investigate how the circuit behaviour depends on temperature.

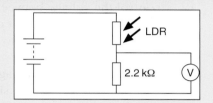

Figure 15.6   Light-sensitive potential divider.

Using an LDR or a thermistor to control voltage

You can use a light-dependent resistor with a fixed resistor to produce a potential divider that is sensitive to light (Figure 15.7). When the LDR is in the dark, its resistance is high and the voltage across it is relatively large. When the LDR is in the light, its resistance is small and the voltage across it is relatively small (Figure 15.8).

The voltage across the fixed resistor in this circuit changes when the resistance of the LDR changes. This is not because the fixed resistor itself has changed, but because the changes in the resistance of the LDR change the current in the circuit.

Similarly, you can use a thermistor with a fixed resistor to produce a potential divider that is sensitive to temperature. When the thermistor is cold, its resistance is high and the voltage across it is relatively large. When the thermistor is hot, its resistance is small and the voltage across it is relatively small.

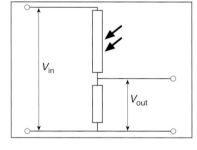

Figure 15.7   When the LDR is dark, its resistance is high.

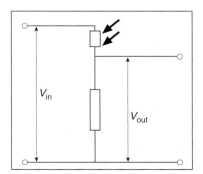

Figure 15.8   When the LDR is in the light, its resistance is low.

16

Voltage–current characteristics

Voltage–current characteristics

Larger voltages across a component push the charge harder, so the current is larger. But the way that the current increases with potential difference varies from component to component. Each component has **V–I characteristics** which show how current varies with voltage.

How does current vary with voltage?

- The simplest variable voltage supply is a battery pack (Figure 16.1). This gives a supply that can be varied in steps of about 1.5 V. You can measure the current for each different voltage.
- You can get a continuously variable voltage by using a potentiometer (Figure 16.2) to control the voltage between zero and maximum.
- For a number of different components, measure the current for a range of voltages.
- Reverse the component to push current in the opposite direction and repeat your readings.
- Draw a graph of current against voltage, including both positive and negative currents and voltages, to show the behaviour of the components.
- For each component, calculate the resistance for a number of values of voltage. Plot a graph of resistance against voltage.

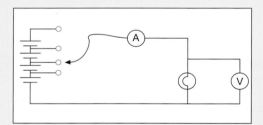

Figure 16.1 *Separate cells can be used to provide a variable voltage.*

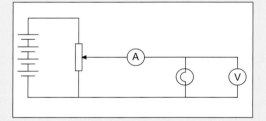

Figure 16.2 *A potentiometer connected to a battery pack can also be used to provide a variable voltage.*

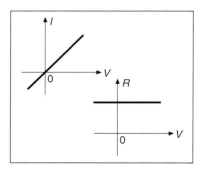

Figure 16.3 *The characteristics of a resistor.*

Ohm's law

All components resist the flow of current in some way or other. You know that the resistance is given by

$$R = \frac{V}{I}$$

For some components, the resistance is constant. So the current through a component is proportional to the voltage across it. This is called **Ohm's law**. Ohm's law applies to many resistors (Figure 16.3) and to many metals at constant temperature. Such components are **ohmic**.

Tungsten filament lamp

For a tungsten filament lamp, the current increases when the voltage increases, but the curve of the graph (Figure 16.4) shows that doubling the voltage produces less than double the current. This is because the filament gets hotter as the current increases and the resistance of the filament increases as it gets hotter.

With care, you can crack the glass of a lamp and measure the characteristics with the filament immersed in water. The filament behaves ohmically and its resistance stays constant, because the temperature stays constant.

Semiconductor diode

The **diode** allows current to flow freely in one direction only (Figure 16.5). This is called the **forward direction**. The current increases rapidly as soon as the forward voltage is greater than about 0.5 V. In the **reverse direction**, very little current flows.

The LED has characteristics that are very similar to an ordinary semiconductor diode, but it needs a greater forward voltage to get the current flowing through it and emits light when it conducts.

Thermistor

Figure 16.6 shows the characteristics of a thermistor with a negative temperature coefficient, which means that its resistance decreases with temperature. It conducts better as the voltage and current get larger; when the voltage doubles, the current more than doubles. The thermistor gets hotter as voltage and current increase, because more power is dissipated in it. The higher temperature frees more charge carriers, and reduces the resistance.

Symmetry

Most electrical components behave symmetrically so that the variation of I with V is the same whichever way round the voltage is connected. Other components, like diodes, are asymmetrical; they behave differently if you reverse the voltage.

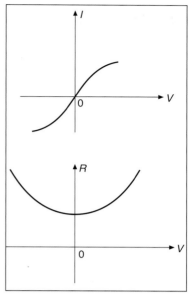

Figure 16.4 The resistance of this lamp increases at higher voltages and currents, because it gets hotter.

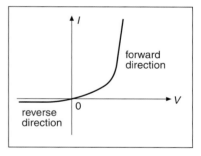

Figure 16.5 This semiconductor diode allows current to flow only in the forward direction.

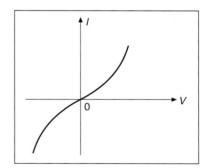

Figure 16.6 A negative-temperature-coefficient thermistor conducts better when V and I become large.

Internal resistance

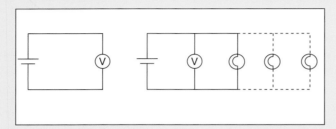
E.m.f., terminal voltage and lost volts

The voltage across the terminals of a cell is called the terminal voltage or **terminal p.d.** If you use a voltmeter that draws very little current to measure the terminal voltage when the cell is supplying no current, the voltmeter measures the cell's e.m.f.

The terminal p.d. of a cell is not constant; it depends on the current you draw from the cell. The larger the current you draw, the smaller the terminal voltage. You lose voltage as the current you draw increases. The **lost volts** is the difference between the e.m.f. and the terminal p.d.

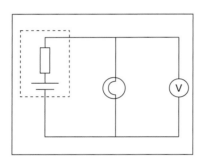

Figure 17.2 All sources of e.m.f. have internal resistance.

Internal resistance

All sources of e.m.f. behave as if they have resistance connected in series with them (Figure 17.2). This resistance is called the **internal resistance**; it is resistance to the flow of current inside the power supply itself.

The internal resistance is part of the total resistance in the circuit. It behaves like any other resistance in the circuit. It needs a voltage across it to push current through it. But internal resistance is part of the power supply, and though you can represent it on a diagram as a separate resistance (Figure 17.3), you cannot get at it to measure it directly. As current flows through the cell, there is a voltage drop across the internal resistance. This voltage drop is the lost volts when you draw current from the cell.

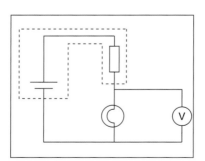

Figure 17.3 It is helpful to consider the internal resistance as part of the external circuit.

Internal resistance

From Kirchhoffs second law, you know that e.m.f. = sum of p.d.s. So from Figure 17.4 you can see that

e.m.f. = lost volts + terminal p.d.

But voltage = current × resistance. So if the internal resistance is r, and the current that flows is I, the lost voltage is equal to Ir. So, if E is the e.m.f. and V is the terminal p.d.

$$E = Ir + V$$

$$V = E - Ir$$

$$V = (-r)I + E$$

If you plot a graph of V against I, this will have slope equal to $-r$ and an intercept of E when $I = 0$.

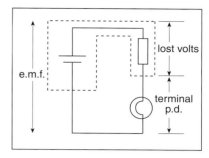

Figure 17.4 E.m.f. = lost volts + terminal p.d.

Measuring internal resistance

- Connect a digital voltmeter alone to a cell to measure the e.m.f.
- Now connect, one at a time, a total of six lamps to the cell. Measure the terminal voltage and current through the cell as shown in Figure 17.5.
- Plot a graph of V against I. Find the internal resistance from the gradient and the e.m.f. from the intercept on the V axis (Figure 17.6).

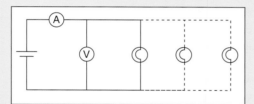

Figure 17.5   Use this circuit to measure internal resistance.

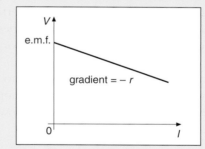

Figure 17.6   Graph of V against I to find internal resistance and e.m.f.

Energy, e.m.f. and terminal voltage

The cell's e.m.f. does work on both the internal resistance and the external load. The **e.m.f.** of the cell is the total work done by the cell (including work done on the internal resistance) per coulomb of charge that flows.

$$\text{e.m.f.} = \frac{\text{total work done}}{\text{charge}}$$

INTERNAL RESISTANCE

Similarly, the terminal voltage or terminal p.d. is the work done on the external circuit per coulomb of charge that flows.

$$\text{terminal p.d.} = \frac{\text{work done on external circuit}}{\text{charge}}$$

The units of e.m.f. and terminal p.d. follow from these definitions. They are joules per coulomb ($J\ C^{-1}$) = volts (V).

Short-circuit current

When you short-circuit a power supply by connecting the terminals together with a low resistance, the only significant resistance in the circuit may be the internal resistance of the power supply (Figure 17.7). In this case

$$\text{current} = \frac{\text{e.m.f.}}{\text{internal resistance}} = \frac{E}{r}$$

For a new 1.5 V AA-size dry cell (Figure 17.8), the short-circuit current may be about 3 A. So the internal resistance

$$r = \frac{E}{I} = \frac{1.5\ \text{V}}{3\ \text{A}} = 0.5\ \Omega$$

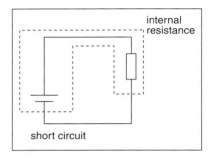

Figure 17.7   The only resistance in this circuit is the internal resistance.

It is safe to short-circuit many small power supplies very briefly, because the internal resistances are usually large enough to prevent damage either to the power supply or to the short-circuiting components. But certain rechargeable cells, such as nickel–cadmium cells and lead–acid car batteries, have very low internal resistances. They can provide dangerously large short-circuit currents.

Usually you want the internal resistance of a power supply to be low, so that it can supply large currents with little energy wasted in the supply. A car battery needs to supply perhaps 200 A. So it needs to have a very low internal resistance indeed.

On the other hand, it is sometimes an advantage to have a large internal resistance, for instance in a high-voltage power supply to prevent it supplying dangerously large currents.

Figure 17.8   The e.m.f. of this AA cell is about 1.5 V. When new, its internal resistance is about 0.5 Ω..

Thermal Physics

Hot and cold. You can feel the difference, but why is it there? Can you measure the difference between a hot and a cold body, and why is there a difference? Why does that cup of tea always cool down, whereas the block of ice melts when you leave them in the same room? So many properties of substances depend on their temperature. Why is that? What does it need to change the temperature of a body? There's more to thermal physics than simply warming your house during winter.

Pressure and temperature

Figure 18.1 Pneumatic systems use air pressure.

Figure 18.2 Hydraulic systems usually use oil as the liquid.

Pneumatic and hydraulic systems

- Put your finger over the end of a plastic syringe and try to compress the air it contains.
- Repeat with the syringe filled with water and then with a piece of wood. What do you observe?
- Connect together plastic syringes of equal size. Feel what happens when you push one syringe. This is a simple example of a pneumatic system (Figure 18.1).
- Repeat the experiment with the syringes filled with water. This is a simple example of a hydraulic system (Figure 18.2).
- Predict what will happen if the syringes are of different cross-sectional areas. Then try it.

Solids and fluids

Solids are **rigid**; they keep their shape. You can use solid objects to transmit forces, along a series of levers, for instance.

Gases and liquids are **fluid**. They flow to fit the shape of their container.

Pressure

When you compress fluids, they exert forces perpendicular to the sides of the containers that constrain them. They exert equal forces on equal areas. So if the area is doubled, the force on it is doubled, but the force per unit area, the **pressure**, stays the same. The size of the pressure is calculated by dividing the (perpendicular) force by the area over which it acts:

$$\text{pressure} = \frac{\text{force}}{\text{area}} \quad \text{or} \quad p = \frac{F}{A}$$

The units of pressure are N m^{-2}, called the pascal (Pa).

Blowing up balloons

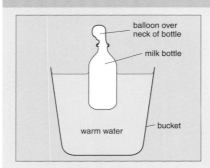

balloon over neck of bottle

milk bottle

warm water

bucket

Figure 18.3 What happens as the temperature of the gas increases?

- Blow a small amount of air into a balloon and note its shape. Blow in some more air. What effect does this have on the balloon? What happens as more and more air is added?
- Blow a small amount of air into a balloon and seal its end. Hold the balloon under the surface of some warm water in a glass bowl. Observe what happens to the balloon. What happens when you remove the balloon from the warm water?
- Fix the neck of a balloon over the top of a milk bottle containing air. Plunge the milk bottle into a bucket of warm water (Figure 18.3). Observe the effect on the balloon.

If you want to investigate how something like the pressure in the balloon changes with temperature, you need a thermometer to make precise temperature measurements. There are many different types of thermometer. One common type uses a liquid rising up a capillary tube – mercury to measure body temperature and alcohol for general measurements. Liquid-crystal thermometers are becoming more common, as are electronic thermometers based on thermocouples (Figure 18.4).

(a)

(b)

(c)

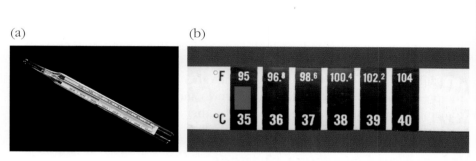

Figure 18.4   Alcohol-in-glass thermometers (a) are common in laboratories, but there are others, including liquid-crystal (b) and thermocouple types (c).

All these thermometers have a substance with a property that changes with temperature. A mercury-in-glass thermometer uses the changing volume of liquid mercury. A thermocouple thermometer uses the changing voltage from a thermocouple. Each of these properties can be used to make a thermometer and to set up a scale of temperature. Before you use a thermometer it has to be marked with a scale, or **calibrated**.

Calibrating a thermocouple thermometer

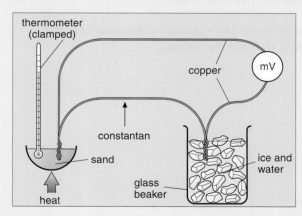

Figure 18.5   One junction of the thermocouple is hot; the other cold.

• A thermocouple has two junctions of different metals. Make a thermocouple thermometer as shown in Figure 18.5 by twisting together a piece of constantan wire with two pieces of copper wire. Temporarily put both junctions in the ice and water mix so that they are both at the same temperature. Measure the voltage.
• Keep one junction in the ice and water and put the other junction in the sand. Measure the voltage from the thermocouple for a range of temperatures of the sand. Plot a graph of voltage against temperature.
• Then use the thermocouple to measure the temperatures of the room, your body, a hot drink and a Bunsen flame.

Macroscopic gas properties

Volume, pressure and temperature

Volume, pressure and temperature are the **macroscopic** (large-scale) **properties** of a gas. They are the properties of the gas that you can observe in the laboratory. The pressure, volume and temperature of a gas are inter-related. If you change one, at least one of the others changes. These properties also depend on the amount of gas present. If you want to find out the connection between the macroscopic properties of a gas, you need to experiment with a fixed amount of gas.

A sealed balloon contains a fixed amount of gas. Its volume increases when it is placed in warm water and the temperature rises. But the pressure changes as well. To investigate gas behaviour, as well as keeping the amount of gas constant, you also need to keep one of the other properties constant (either the pressure, the volume or the temperature) and investigate how the remaining two properties depend on each other.

Volume and pressure changes

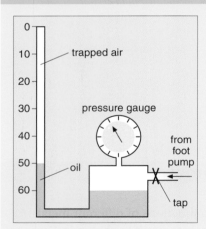

Figure 19.1   *The volume decreases when the pressure increases.*

- The oil in the closed tube traps a fixed mass of air (Figure 19.1). If the column of air has a constant cross-section, its length is proportional to its volume. Measure the length of this column and record the corresponding pressure.
- Use the foot pump to increase the pressure acting on the trapped air. Allow a few moments for the temperature of the trapped air to return to room temperature. Record the new volume and pressure readings.
- Repeat for six more values of pressure. Plot a graph of pressure against volume.
- Multiply each pressure by its corresponding volume and compare results.
- How would you use the pressure and volume readings to obtain a graph that is a straight line through the origin?

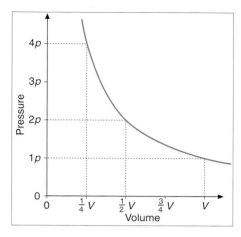

Figure 19.2   Pressure is inversely proportional to volume.

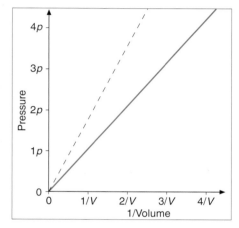

Figure 19.3   Pressure is proportional to 1/volume.

Boyle's law

The volume of a gas decreases as the pressure acting on it increases. The **isothermal** (constant-temperature) curve of Figure 19.2 shows that the volume halves when the pressure doubles, and that it quarters when the pressure increases fourfold. The product (pressure × volume) remains the same:

$$\text{pressure } p \times \text{ volume } V = \text{pressure } 2p \times \text{ volume } \tfrac{1}{2}V$$
$$= \text{pressure } 4p \times \text{ volume } \tfrac{1}{4}V$$

Boyle's law states that:

> **For a fixed mass of gas at constant temperature, the product of the pressure and volume is constant.**

Since

$$\text{pressure} \times \text{volume} = \text{constant}$$

we get

$$\text{pressure} = \frac{\text{constant}}{\text{volume}}$$

or

$$\text{pressure} \propto \frac{1}{\text{volume}}$$

Pressure and volume are inversely proportional to each other. A graph of pressure against 1/volume is a straight line through the origin (Figure 19.3).

The dashed line in Figure 19.3 represents the behaviour of the same mass of gas at a higher constant temperature. How would a higher temperature affect the isothermal curve in Figure 19.2?

WORKED EXAMPLE

The cylinder of a pump contains $100\,cm^3$ of air at atmospheric pressure ($100\,000\,Pa$). The piston is pushed in until the volume of the air is reduced by $20\,cm^3$. The air cools back to its original temperature. Calculate the new pressure of the air in the cylinder.

We use the equation

$$\text{pressure} \times \text{volume} = \text{constant}$$

to find the value of the constant from the initial values for pressure and volume:

$$100\,000\,Pa \times 100\,cm^3 = 1 \times 10^7\,Pa\,cm^3$$

We then use the equation again with the new pressure and new volume:

$$\text{new pressure} \times \text{new volume} = 1 \times 10^7\,Pa\,cm^3$$

We have a new volume of $100\,cm^3 - 20\,cm^3 = 80\,cm^3$ so the new values give

$$\text{new pressure} = \frac{1 \times 10^7\,Pa\,cm^3}{\text{new volume}} = \frac{1 \times 10^7\,Pa\,cm^3}{80\,cm^3} = 125\,000\,Pa$$

The ideal gas equation

Pressure and temperature

- Assemble the apparatus shown in Figure 20.1 and make sure that as much of the flask as possible is submerged in the water bath. Why is it important to use a *short* length of rubber tubing to connect the flask to the pressure gauge?
- Vary the temperature of the water bath by adding ice or heating with the Bunsen burner. Observe the changes to the reading of the pressure gauge. For a range of temperatures, record a series of corresponding readings of the pressure of the gas in the flask and the temperature of the water bath. For each pair of readings, keep the temperature of the water bath steady and allow time for the gas to reach the same temperature.
- Plot a graph of pressure against temperature. Then plot another graph to predict the temperature at which the pressure would become zero.

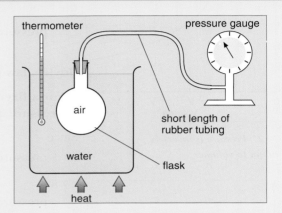

Figure 20.1 As the temperature increases, the gas pressure increases.

The pressure law

A graph of pressure against Celsius temperature is a straight line but it does not pass through the origin (Figure 20.2). The pressure is not zero at 0 °C, so pressure is not directly proportional to the Celsius temperature.

If you extrapolate (extend) the graph to lower temperatures as in Figure 20.3, it eventually cuts the temperature axis at approximately –273 °C. This is the temperature at which the graph predicts that the pressure would become zero. Experiments with different amounts of gas, and different gases, all predict the same temperature for zero pressure. This temperature is called **absolute zero**, the lowest temperature possible.

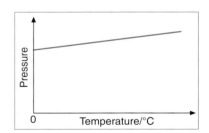

Figure 20.2 Gas pressure increases linearly with temperature.

The Kelvin scale (also called the absolute scale) of temperature *starts* at absolute zero. Figure 20.4 shows the Kelvin scale side by side with the Celsius scale. Zero kelvin (0 K) is –273 °C. The ice point, 0 °C, is 273 K. To find the Kelvin temperature, add 273 K to the Celsius temperature. It is usual to use the symbol T for Kelvin temperature, and θ for Celsius temperature. So

$$T/\text{K} = \theta/°\text{C} + 273$$

Figure 20.3 The graph predicts that the pressure would be zero at –273 °C.

The graph of pressure against Kelvin temperature is a straight line through the origin. So pressure is proportional to Kelvin temperature. The **pressure law** states that:

For a fixed mass of gas at constant volume, the pressure is directly proportional to the Kelvin temperature.

Since pressure ∝ Kelvin temperature we can write

$$p \propto T \quad \text{or} \quad p = \text{constant} \times T$$

$$\frac{p}{T} = \text{constant}$$

An ideal gas

All gases will liquefy in the right circumstances. You can liquefy a few gases just by raising the pressure, but for most gases you have to reduce the temperature as well. Each gas has a **critical temperature**: below a gas's critical temperature you can liquefy the gas by applying sufficient pressure; above a gas's critical temperature you cannot liquefy the gas at all.

If you compare the behaviour of different gases at modest (around atmospheric) pressures and well above their critical temperatures, you find that they behave similarly and follow closely Boyle's law and the pressure law. It is useful to think of an **ideal gas**, which would obey the gas laws at all temperatures and pressures. An ideal gas like this would have perfect properties to define the Kelvin scale of temperature.

Figure 20.5 shows a thermometer that uses a constant volume, and constant mass, of gas **(a constant-volume gas thermometer)**.
So the gas pressure is proportional to the Kelvin temperature.

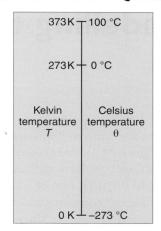

Figure 20.4 Kelvin temperature = Celsius temperature + 273K.

The ideal gas equation

Gas pressure is proportional to Kelvin temperature, so pressure divided by Kelvin temperature is constant. Boyle's law states that pressure multiplied by volume is a constant. These two equations may be combined as:

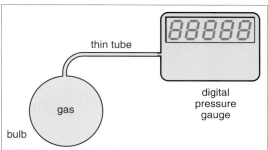

Figure 20.5 Constant-volume gas thermometer. Temperature is defined as being proportional to the pressure of the gas.

$$\frac{pV}{T} = \text{constant} \quad \text{or} \quad \frac{p_1 V_1}{T_1} = \frac{p_2 V_2}{T_2}$$

The value of the constant depends on how much gas is present. For one mole of gas (6.023×10^{23} molecules) this constant is R, the *molar gas constant*:

$$\frac{pV}{T} = R \qquad \text{for one mole of gas}$$

The volume of one mole of any gas at atmospheric pressure ($101\,400\,\text{N}\,\text{m}^{-2}$) and a temperature of $0°C$ ($273\,\text{K}$) is $0.0224\,\text{m}^3$. From this you can calculate R:

$$R = \frac{pV}{T} = \frac{101\,400\ \text{N}\,\text{m}^{-2} \times 0.224\ \text{m}^3}{273\ \text{K}} = 8.3\,\text{N}\,\text{m}\,\text{K}^{-1} = 8.3\,\text{J}\,\text{K}^{-1}$$

A mass m of gas contains m/M moles, where M is the **molar mass** (the mass of a mole). So for a mass m,

$$\frac{pV}{T} = \left(\frac{m}{M}\right)R \quad \text{or} \quad pV = \left(\frac{m}{M}\right)RT$$

This equation is called the **ideal gas equation**.

Modelling the behaviour of a gas

Observing smoke

- Use the lamp to illuminate the glass tube (Figure 21.1): the glass rod acts as a lens and focuses light from the lamp inside the tube.
- Hold the unlit end of a burning straw above the tube. Close the container and trap some smoke inside.
- Observe the smoke through a microscope. Smoke particles appear as very small bright dots. They reflect light from the lamp into the microscope. What are the smoke particles doing? What makes them behave in this way?

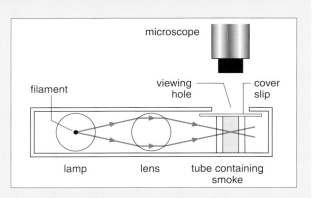

Figure 21.1 The tube contains smoke.

Brownian motion

Smoke consists of small particles suspended in the air. You can see the particles under a microscope. They dance about randomly, moving first one way and then immediately another. The motion of the smoke particles that you can see in the school laboratory experiment above is due to turbulence (disturbance) of the air. But even if you take special care to make sure that the air is still, you can still see random motion of the smoke particles. A botanist, Robert Brown, first saw similar movement when he observed pollen grains in water and gave his name to this random, zigzag motion.

Brownian motion of the smoke particles provides evidence that air consists of particles moving randomly at high speeds. The visible smoke particles are being knocked about by invisible air molecules hitting them. Smoke particles are small and light. The small size means that there will nearly always be more air molecules hitting one side than another at any instant (Figure 21.2). So there will be a resultant force pushing the particle in different directions from moment to moment. The very low mass means that the constantly changing resultant force is sufficient to move the particle, as seen by the microscope.

Smoke particles are small, but air molecules are very much smaller. Air molecules must be moving at very high speeds to have sufficient momentum to cause the heavier smoke particles to move with Brownian motion.

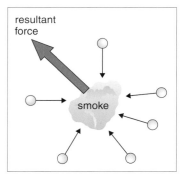

Figure 21.2 At a given instant, the forces on the smoke particle are unbalanced.

Modelling a gas

- In the model of a gas shown in Figure 21.3, small ball bearings represent air molecules. Unlike air molecules, their collisions are not elastic, so the motor is needed to keep them moving.
- Increase the speed of the motor to make the molecules move faster. What happens to the volume, indicated by the height of the cardboard disc?
- Add mass to the cardboard disc. What effect does this have on the volume?
- Then remove the cardboard disc. Observe the distribution of the ball bearings.
- Place a small polystyrene sphere (representing a smoke particle) in with the ball bearings. Switch on the motor and observe the Brownian motion of the sphere.

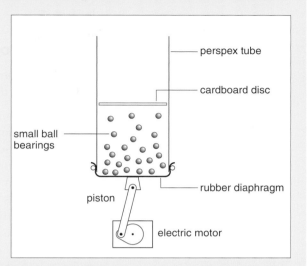

Figure 21.3 The ball bearings represent gas molecules.

Gas laws and the mechanical model

The collisions of the ball bearings with the cardboard disc exert a force on it. In a similar way, the molecules of a gas exert a force on the walls of their container as they collide with it. Faster movement of the ball bearings corresponds to an increase in temperature.

If you keep the volume occupied by the ball bearings constant and increase their speed, the ball bearings hit the container walls harder and more frequently, producing an increased pressure. This corresponds to the pressure law.

If the cardboard disc is free to rise, an increase in the speed of the ball bearings will produce an increase in volume. The pressure exerted by the molecules remains the same. They hit the sides of the container harder, but less often.

Adding weight to the cardboard disc increases the pressure and reduces the volume. This increases the packing density of its molecules (Figure 21.4). The number of collisions made with the walls increases and produces a greater pressure. This corresponds to Boyle's law.

The ball bearings in our model stop moving when the motor is turned off. They soon lose their kinetic energy – their collisions are *inelastic*. The average kinetic energy of gas molecules in a constant-temperature enclosure remains the same. The molecules do not lose their kinetic energy – their collisions are *elastic*.

The atmosphere is denser near the Earth; its molecules are further apart at greater heights. When you remove the cardboard disk, gravity keeps the ball bearings in the tube. The ball bearings are more densely packed at the bottom of the cylinder, where they exert a greater pressure, and thin out with height.

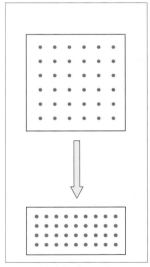

Figure 21.4 Halving the volume doubles the packing density.

Kinetic theory of an ideal gas

Assumptions about gas molecules

Experimental observation led physicists to make some assumptions about gases, which led to a theoretical model of a gas.

- From Brownian motion they assumed that a pure gas consists of identical molecules in continuous random motion.
- Molecules never come to a stop and settle at the bottom of the container, so they assumed that molecular collisions are on average elastic.
- You can compress a gas a lot, so they assumed that the volume of the molecules is negligible compared with the volume of the container.
- Therefore, the molecules must be a relatively long way apart, so they assumed that there are no forces on the molecules except during collisions.

A theoretical model of a gas

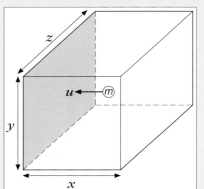

Figure 22.1 shows a box whose sides are of length x, y and z. A single gas molecule, mass m, is bouncing between the shaded face and its opposite one with speed u. Taking rightwards as positive, the momentum of the molecule *after* colliding with the left-hand face is $+mu$; *before* the collision it was $-mu$ (Figure 22.2). So

change of momentum = final momentum – initial momentum
$$= +mu - (-mu) = 2mu$$

The molecule travels a distance $2x$ between collisions with the *shaded* face:

$$\text{time between collisions} = \frac{\text{distance}}{\text{speed}} = \frac{2x}{u}$$

Figure 22.1 A single gas molecule, mass m, is bouncing between the shaded face and its opposite with speed u.

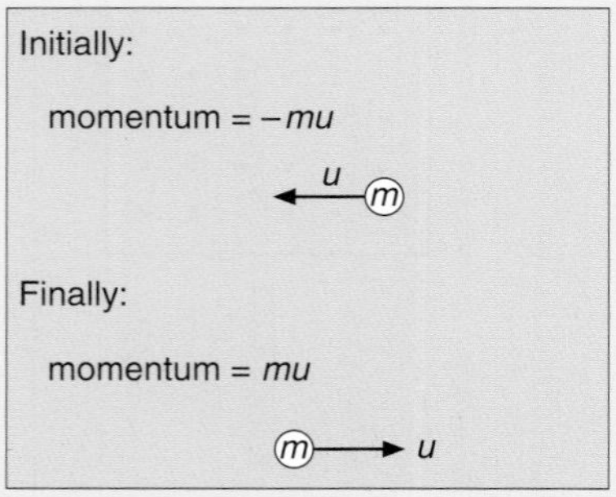

Force exerted on shaded wall by molecule = rate of change of momentum:

$$\text{force} = \frac{(\text{change of momentum})}{\text{time}} = \frac{2mu}{2x/u} = \frac{mu^2}{x}$$

We can now find the pressure exerted by the single molecule on the shaded face:

Initially:

momentum $= -mu$

$\xleftarrow{u} \text{\textcircled{m}}$

Finally:

momentum $= mu$

$\text{\textcircled{m}} \xrightarrow{} u$

$$\text{pressure} = \frac{\text{force}}{\text{area}} = \frac{mu^2/x}{yz} = \frac{mu^2}{xyz}$$

But xyz = volume V of the box, so for a single molecule

$$\text{pressure} = \frac{mu^2}{V}$$

Figure 22.2 Change of momentum = mu – (–mu) = 2mu.

In a real box of gas, there are N molecules moving randomly. You can assume that, on average, only a third of these are colliding with the shaded face and its opposite, and a third on each of the other pairs of faces. The molecules do not all move at the same speed u, but have a range of speeds, and their average or mean square speed is written as $\langle c^2 \rangle$. Therefore

$$\text{total pressure } p = \tfrac{1}{3}N\frac{m\langle c^2 \rangle}{V} \quad \text{so} \quad pV = \tfrac{1}{3}Nm\langle c^2 \rangle$$

Root mean square speed

The product $N \times m$ is the total mass of gas in the box. $\dfrac{Nm}{V}$ gives the density ρ. So the previous equation can be written

$$p = \tfrac{1}{3}\rho\langle c^2 \rangle$$

Atmospheric pressure is about 100 kPa and the density of air is about $1\,\text{kg}\,\text{m}^{-3}$. Using these values we can find the mean square speed of air molecules:

$$\langle c^2 \rangle = \frac{3p}{\rho} = \frac{3 \times 100\,000\,\text{Pa}}{1\,\text{kg m}^{-3}} = 300\,000\,\text{m}^2\text{s}^{-2}$$

The **root mean square (r.m.s.) speed** is the square root of the mean square speed, where the mean square speed is the sum of the squares of the molecular speeds divided by the total number of molecules. For the air molecules:

$$\textbf{r.m.s. speed} = \sqrt{(300\,000\,\text{m}^2\text{s}^{-2})} = 550\,\text{m}\,\text{s}^{-1}$$

It is not surprising that the speed of sound, about $340\,\text{m}\,\text{s}^{-1}$, is comparable with this, since the molecules convey the sound waves.

Molecular speed and temperature

For one mole of gas, the equation $pV = \tfrac{1}{3}Nm\langle c^2 \rangle$ becomes

$$pV = \tfrac{1}{3}N_{\text{A}}m\langle c^2 \rangle$$

where N_{A} is the *Avogadro constant*, the number of molecules in one mole. So

$$pV = \tfrac{2}{3}N_{\text{A}} \times \tfrac{1}{2}m\langle c^2 \rangle$$

where $\tfrac{1}{2}m\langle c^2 \rangle$ is the mean kinetic energy of a single molecule. This equation has to agree with the ideal gas equation for one mole of gas, $pV = RT$. So

$$\tfrac{2}{3}N_{\text{A}} \times \tfrac{1}{2}m\langle c^2 \rangle = RT \quad \text{or} \quad \tfrac{1}{2}m\langle c^2 \rangle = \tfrac{3}{2}\left(\frac{R}{N_{\text{A}}}\right)T$$

$\dfrac{R}{N_{\text{A}}}$, the molar gas constant divided by the Avogadro constant, is the gas constant per molecule, known as the *Boltzmann constant k*, where

$$k = \frac{R}{N_{\text{A}}} = \frac{8.3\,\text{J K}^{-1}\,\text{mol}^{-1}}{6.02 \times 10^{23}\,\text{mol}^{-1}} = 1.38 \times 10^{-23}\,\text{J K}^{-1}$$

$$\text{So} \quad \tfrac{1}{2}m\langle c^2 \rangle = \tfrac{3}{2}kT$$

This equation states that the average molecular kinetic energy is proportional to the **Kelvin temperature**. This equation is now used to define temperature as that quantity which is proportional to the molecular kinetic energy of an ideal gas.

Distribution of molecular speeds

Although the air molecules around you have an r.m.s. speed of $550\,\text{m}\,\text{s}^{-1}$, at a given instant some of them will be almost stationary whereas others will be moving at over three times this value.

Figure 22.3 shows the distribution of speeds in the molecules of a gas. Graph A shows the distribution for a lower temperature, T_1. Graph B shows the distribution for the same amount of gas at a higher temperature, T_2.

The area under the curve is proportional to the number of molecules. So both graphs A and B have the same area.

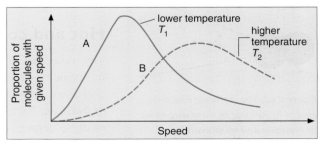

Figure 22.3 At higher temperatures the mean speed of the molecules increases, although the proportion of the molecules in a given range around this particular speed is less.

Internal energy

Internal energy

You studied internal energy in Chapter 30 of *Mechanics and Radioactivity*. In the previous two chapters of this book you have learned about the way that the molecules inside a gas behave. You can put these two pieces of physics together to understand what internal energy is.

The molecules of a gas are moving around. Molecules with more than one atom can also spin and vibrate. All these movements can store kinetic energy.

If you could look inside a gas, you might occasionally see two molecules heading directly towards each other, slowing down, stopping, and then springing away from each other as shown in Figure 23.1.

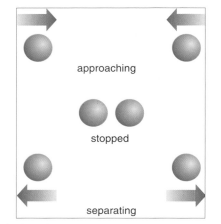

Figure 23.1 *When the molecules are stationary, all the energy is potential.*

What has happened to the kinetic energy of those molecules? As the molecules get close, there are repulsive forces between them. At the point where both molecules are stationary, all their kinetic energy has been converted into potential energy stored by doing work against the repulsive forces between the molecules.

When the molecules in a gas are colliding, they are working against these repulsive forces and there is a continual interchange between kinetic and potential energy.

The random kinetic and potential energy inside a gas is its **internal energy**. If you raise the temperature of the gas, the molecules move faster and approach closer when they collide; they have more random kinetic and potential energy. So raising the temperature of a body raises its internal energy.

The internal energy of other bodies is also the sum of the molecular kinetic and potential energies. In a solid, the molecules cannot move around, but they are vibrating, constantly swapping kinetic energy for potential energy and vice versa.

In a liquid the motion of the molecules is somewhere in between the behaviour of a solid and a gas, but, just the same, the kinetic and potential energy of its molecules make up the internal energy of the liquid.

Hot and cold bodies

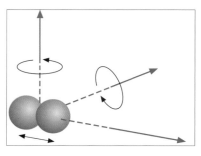

Figure 23.2 *The molecule can store energy by moving in three directions, by rotating and by vibrating.*

The molecules of a body act as tiny stores of kinetic and potential energy. Each molecule has a number of independent ways of moving – from side to side, up and down, rotating, vibrating and so on (Figure 23.2). These are called *degrees of freedom*. Each degree of freedom can store energy, and together the energy of these degrees of freedom make up the internal energy of the body.

In a hot body, each degree of freedom has, on average, a large amount of energy. In a cold body, each degree of freedom has, on average, a small amount of energy.

The energy in a body is spread randomly amongst the degrees of freedom. Also, the distribution of the energy changes as it shuffles about randomly from one degree of freedom to another.

Figure 23.3 represents the degrees of freedom of two bodies as a number of boxes. The dots each represent a unit of energy. In the hot body B, each degree of freedom has, on average, 2 units of energy. But you can see that at one instant any one degree of freedom might have 0, 1, 2, 3 units of energy, or even more. Only on average will it have 2 units. The cold body A has an average of 1 unit of energy per degree of freedom.

Heating

If you put a hot body (large amount of energy per degree of freedom) in thermal contact with a cold body (small amount of energy per degree of freedom), then the energy shuffles randomly between the two bodies. Sometimes energy goes from the hot body to the cold body; and sometimes energy goes from the cold body to the hot body. But on average, since there is more energy per degree of freedom in the hot body, energy goes from the hot body to the cold body.

Random shuffling of quanta like this eventually results in the energy evening out, so that both bodies have the same average amount of energy per degree of freedom – they both have the same temperature. Figure 23.4 shows the bodies of Figure 23.3 after they have been in contact for a while. On average, both sides have 1.5 units of energy per degree of freedom.

Oscillating molecules

The internal energy of a solid depends on the energy of its vibrating molecules. The molecules sometimes have kinetic energy and sometimes have potential energy. On average, half their energy is kinetic and half is potential. So the internal energy of a solid has both kinetic and potential energy components. If you increase the temperature of a solid, you increase both the kinetic energy and the potential energy of the molecules.

The internal energy of gases

You read in Chapter 22 that temperature is defined as that quantity which is proportional to the molecular kinetic energy of an ideal gas. Atomic potential energy is due to forces between the atoms. In an ideal monatomic gas, there are no forces between the atoms, so there is no atomic or molecular potential energy. So the internal energy of an ideal gas is only kinetic and temperature is proportional to the internal energy, i.e. the kinetic energy of an ideal gas.

In real gases, there are forces between the atoms and molecules. So the internal energy of a real gas is both potential and kinetic.

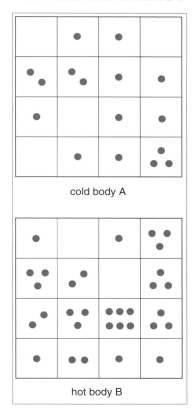

Figure 23.3 The hot body has more energy per degree of freedom.

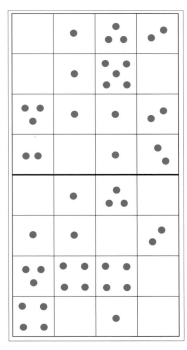

Figure 23.4 When you put hot and cold bodies into contact, the distribution of energy evens out.

Steady state and thermal equilibrium

Good and bad conductors

Thermal conduction is the flow of internal energy through a material that does not move. Some materials are good thermal conductors. Diamond is a good conductor: internal energy can move rapidly through the regularly and rigidly fastened atoms. Metals are good conductors because electrons inside them can move freely and take energy with them. Glass, with its irregular structure, less-rigid bonds and absence of free electrons, is a poor conductor.

Convection

Convection takes place when a medium moves and takes internal energy with it. Natural convection takes place when the temperature of a gas or a liquid is uneven. Where the fluid is hotter, it is less dense. So the upthrust from the surrounding colder fluid is greater than the weight of the warm fluid. There is then a net upward force which pushes the warm fluid up.

Thermal equilibrium

If you place a hot object in contact with a cold one, the hot object will give energy to the cold one, and the cold object will receive energy from the hot one. Eventually they will reach the same temperature. They are then in **thermal equilibrium**.

When you put a cold thermometer in contact with a hot object. It takes some time for the temperature of the thermometer to rise to that of the hot object. During this process, the temperature of the hot object will fall. Eventually the thermometer and the object will reach the same temperature as each other. They are then in thermal equilibrium. Only then will the thermometer indicate the true temperature of the object.

You need to wait for thermal equilibrium between a thermometer and an object before measuring temperature.

When the two bodies have reached the same temperature, energy shuffling still takes place. But now, since both bodies have the same amount of energy per degree of freedom, on average there is no net flow of energy from one to the other. Energy flows from A to B and from B to A at the same rate. The two bodies are in thermal equilibrium with no net energy flow and, as you read in Chapter 23, their temperatures are the same.

Thermal equilibrium is a *dynamic* equilibrium. Energy is constantly being exchanged between the bodies, but the *net* transfer is zero. In a *static* equilibrium there would be no transfer of energy at all.

Heat transfer

If one body is in contact with another body at a different temperature, then energy flows from the hot body to the cold body.

The flow of internal energy like this, caused by a temperature difference, is called **heat** or **heat transfer**. Heat transfer is a random process in which energy drifts from hot to cold.

Radiation

You will study electromagnetic radiation in *Waves and our Universe*. Electromagnetic radiation is emitted from bodies at all temperatures, but the intensity is greater with increasing temperature. The electromagnetic quanta transfer energy at the speed of light. When another body absorbs them, they raise its internal energy (Figure 24.1).

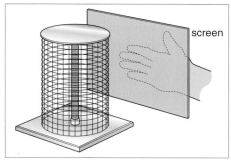

Figure 24.1 Remove the screen and notice how quickly your hand gets hot.

Keeping warm

In the British climate, for much of the year our surroundings are at a colder temperature than we, personally, would like to be. Our body temperature is about 37°C and, when clothed, we are comfortable in surroundings that are about 20°C. But the outdoor temperatures are usually less than that. So, for much of the year, we keep our homes at higher temperatures than the outside.

When the insides of our houses are hotter than the outsides, internal energy flows outwards through the walls (Figure 24.2). If we want to keep the insides warm, we need continuously to make up for this loss. This is the function of home heating.

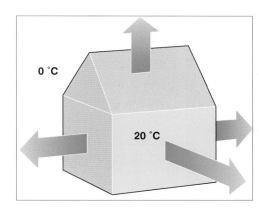

Figure 24.2 When the outside is colder than the inside of your house, energy leaks out.

Steady state

Though inside and outside temperatures change, there are some parts of the day when you can regard the inside temperature as constant, perhaps at 20°C, and the outside temperature as constant, perhaps at 10°C. If these temperatures remain steady for some time, the temperature of the structure of the building becomes steady. The temperatures across the bricks have become constant, with, perhaps, a temperature in the middle of 15°C, half-way between the inside and outside temperatures. This situation is known as **steady state**. There is steady flow of internal energy from the inside of the house to the outside, but all temperatures are remaining constant.

Steady state is quite different from thermal equilibrium. In thermal equilibrium, all the temperatures are the same. There is no net flow of internal energy at all. In steady state, the temperatures are constant but different, and there are steady flows of internal energy (Table 24.3).

Table 24.3 *The difference between steady state and thermal equilibrium*

Steady state	Thermal equilibrium
Objects are at *different constant* temperatures	Objects are all at the *same* temperature
There is a steady flow of energy by heating	There is no net flow of energy by heating

25 Specific heat capacity

Heating water

- Put 100 g of water in a lagged plastic beaker with a heater and a thermometer (Figure 25.1). Measure the starting temperature. Supply 1000 J of energy to the water, measured with a joulemeter. Stir the water and measure the final temperature.
- Add energy in further 1000 J steps until the temperature has risen by about 15 K. Plot a graph of temperature rise against energy supplied.
- Repeat the experiment with 200 g of water. What differences do you observe?

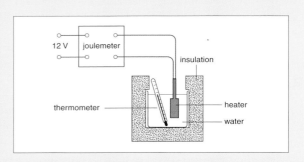

Figure 25.1 *The joulemeter measures the energy supplied.*

Specific heat capacity

Table 25.1 *Some specific heat capacities*

Material	Specific heat capacity ($J\,kg^{-1}\,K^{-1}$)
lead	130
copper	380
iron	450
aluminium	880
concrete block	920
water	4200

If you raise the temperature of an object, you increase the kinetic energy of its molecules—you increase its internal energy. So you need to supply energy. The energy needed to raise the temperature of an object is proportional to the increase in temperature and the mass of the object

$$energy \propto mass \times temperature\ rise$$

The constant of proportionality depends on the substance you are heating. It is called the **specific heat capacity** c (Table 25.1). So

$$energy = mass \times specific\ heat\ capacity \times temperature\ rise$$
$$energy = mc\Delta T$$

so that $$c = \frac{energy}{m\Delta T}$$

The units of specific heat capacity are $\dfrac{J}{kg\,K} = J\,kg^{-1}\,K^{-1}$.

The specific heat capacity is sometimes called the *specific enthalpy*.

Measuring the specific heat capacity of aluminium

- Take an aluminium block drilled to take a heater and thermometer and measure its mass. Lag the block and insert the heater and thermometer (Figure 25.2). Measure the initial temperature.
- Turn the heater on for 2 min and measure the voltage and current. Continue to measure the temperature after you turn the heater off and record the highest temperature reached.
- Calculate the energy supplied = voltage × current × time.
- Divide the energy by the mass and the temperature rise to calculate the specific heat capacity.

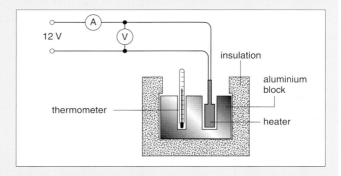

Figure 25.2 *Measure voltage, current and time to calculate the energy supplied.*

Sources of experimental error

There are significant sources of experimental error in both experiments to measure specific heat capacity. One error is associated with the measurement of the temperature rise. When heating water, it is comparatively easy to ensure that the temperature of the water is even, by continual stirring. It is harder to measure the temperature of a metal block accurately, because the parts near the heater will be hotter than the parts further away.

Another source of error is the energy supplied by the power supply that does not end up inside the material whose specific heat capacity you are measuring. Some energy supplied is used to raise the temperature of the heater itself, and the thermometer and some energy leaks away through the insulation to the surrounding room.

To minimise these errors:
- Insulate the apparatus well to minimise energy loss.
- Use thermometers and heaters whose mass is small in comparison with the mass of the material being investigated, so that most of the energy goes to this material.
- After you have supplied a known amount of energy, turn the power supply off but keep measuring the temperature. Record the highest temperature. This gives the extra energy remaining in the heater when the power supply was switched off time to spread throughout the apparatus.

Specific heat capacity and the mass of molecules

A copper atom is much more massive than an aluminium atom. This means that a kilogram of copper has many fewer atoms than a kilogram of aluminium. Each atom of copper or aluminium needs about the same energy for each $1\,K$ rise in temperature. It is easier to raise the temperature of $1\,kg$ of copper through $1\,K$ than to raise the temperature of $1\,kg$ of aluminium by the same amount. The specific heat capacity of copper is about $380\,J\,kg^{-1}K^{-1}$; that of aluminium is about $880\,J\,kg^{-1}K^{-1}$. You can see from Table 25.1 that materials with massive molecules have low specific heat capacities.

Electric storage heaters store internal energy. They receive energy from the electricity supply during the night (when it is cheaper!) and give it out during the day. Storage heaters are heavy: they need a large mass to store a large amount of internal energy. But their designers want to minimise their mass. For a given temperature rise, a substance with a high specific heat capacity can store more energy per kilogram. So storage heaters use materials of high specific heat capacity – generally concrete blocks. Though the blocks have only a quarter of the specific heat capacity of water, they can be raised through a much higher temperature, and therefore store more energy per kilogram.

WORKED EXAMPLE

The specific heat capacity of water is $4200\,J\,kg^{-1}K^{-1}$. Calculate the energy needed to raise a kettle-full of water, volume 1.4 litres, from tap temperature, 10 °C, to boiling point.

The density of water is $1.0\,kg\,l^{-1}$ and so the mass of 1.4 litres of water is 1.4 kg. To find the energy needed, we use

$$\text{energy} = \text{mass} \times \text{specific heat capacity} \times \text{temperature rise}$$

$$= 1.4\,kg \times 4200\,J\,kg^{-1}K^{-1} \times (100 - 10)\,K = 0.53\,MJ$$

Energy costs about 2p per megajoule from the electricity supply. So the cost of heating this kettle-full of water is about 1.06p.

Specific latent heat

Measuring the energy required to boil away water

- Put a measuring cylinder on a top pan balance and surround the cylinder with lagging. Support a heater as shown in Figure 26.1. Fill the measuring cylinder with boiling water and turn on the power supply. Wait until the water comes back to the boil.
- Measure the voltage and current supplied to the heater. Then time how long it takes to boil away 5 g of water.
- Calculate the energy required to boil away 1 kg of water.

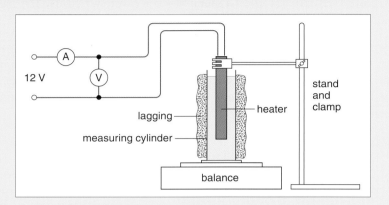

12 V

stand
and
clamp

heater

lagging

measuring cylinder

balance

Figure 26.1 The heater boils away the water.

Specific latent heat

You need energy to turn a liquid into a vapour. The energy is used to tear the molecules apart, greatly increasing their potential energy. The energy required to turn 1 kg of a particular liquid to vapour at the same temperature is called its **specific latent heat of vaporisation** L.

To vaporise a given mass of a substance:

energy = mass × specific latent heat of vaporisation

energy = mL

You also need energy to turn a solid into a liquid. Again, the energy is used to increase the potential energy of the molecules, releasing the molecules from their fixed positions, but not freeing them from their neighbours completely. The energy required to turn 1 kg of a particular solid to liquid at the same temperature is called its **specific latent heat of fusion** L.

To melt a given mass of a substance:

energy = mass × specific latent heat of fusion

energy = mL

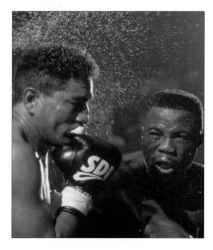

Figure 26.2 We sweat to lower our temperature.

When we get hot, we sweat, as Figure 26.2 shows. The sweat needs energy, its latent heat of vaporisation, to evaporate. It takes that from the body and cools the body down.

Measuring the specific latent heat of fusion of water

- Set up two funnels filled with crushed ice as shown in Figure 26.3. Put a heater (not yet turned on) in one of the funnels and leave them both for a minute so the heater reaches the temperature of the ice.
- Turn on the heater and record the voltage and current supplied. Catch the water melted from each funnel in a time of 2 min and measure its mass. Subtract the mass of water collected from the funnel without the heater from that collected from the funnel with the heater, to find the extra mass of ice melted by the heater.
- Why is some ice melted in the funnel without the heater? Why do you subtract this from the mass melted in the other funnel?
- Calculate the energy supplied to the heater and divide it by the mass of ice melted by the heater to find the specific latent heat of fusion of ice (water) in J kg^{-1}.

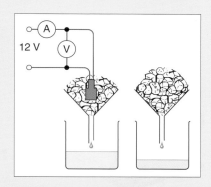

Figure 26.3 More ice melts in the side with the heater.

WORKED EXAMPLE

A kettle has an element with a power of 2.2 kW. When full of water, it remains turned on for 2 min after the water reaches boiling point. The specific latent heat of vaporisation of water is 2.3 MJ kg^{-1}. Calculate the mass of water boiled off.

Energy supplied is given by

$$\text{energy} = \text{power} \times \text{time} = 2200\,\text{W} \times 120\,\text{s} = 264\,000\,\text{J} = 0.264\,\text{MJ}$$

Mass of water boiled off is found from

$$\text{energy} = \text{mass vaporised} \times \text{specific latent heat of vaporisation}$$

so

$$\text{mass vaporised} = \frac{\text{energy}}{\text{specific latent heat of vaporisation}}$$

$$= \frac{0.264\,\text{MJ}}{2.3\,\text{MJ kg}^{-1}} = 0.115\,\text{kg} = 115\,\text{g}$$

Of course, not all of the 2.2 kW being supplied is being used to boil the water. Some of it is being lost to the surroundings by conduction, convection and radiation. So, in practice, the amount boiled off in 2 min will be less than 115 g.

Enthalpy

As stated above, you increase the potential energy of the molecules when you change a solid to a liquid, or a liquid to its vapour. You therefore increase the internal energy of the substance. If the surrounding pressure is constant during these changes of state, the substance will change volume – usually expanding when going from solid to liquid or from liquid to vapour. As you can read in more detail in the next chapter, this means that the substance does work on its surroundings.

Therefore, the energy supplied for a change of state is partly used to increase the internal energy of the substance involved and partly to work on the surroundings. This energy supplied is called the *enthalpy*. For this reason, the specific latent heat is sometimes called the **specific enthalpy**.

So for a change of state from liquid to gas you could write:

enthalpy supplied = mass × specific enthalpy of vaporisation

Heating and working

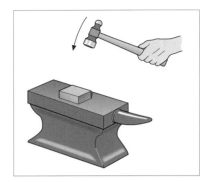

Figure 27.1 *Beat the lead block and observe the change in temperature.*

Working mechanically on a lead block

- Take a block of lead at room temperature. Use a hammer to beat it on a firm and solid base for a few minutes (Figure 27.1). Then measure its temperature.
- What has happened to the internal energy of the block?

Mechanical working

When you squash a lead block, you apply a force to it which moves in the direction of the force. You are doing work on the block. This is **mechanical working**. The lead is hard to distort; you need large forces to compress it a small distance. You can calculate the work done by multiplying the average force by the distance moved in the direction of the force (Figure 27.2):

$$\text{work} = \text{force} \times \text{distance} \quad \text{or} \quad \Delta W = F\Delta x$$

To work on the block, you need energy. You become tired and have less. What has happened to the energy?

The energy has not simply disappeared; it is inside the lead block. If you could examine the lead block microscopically after squashing, you would find that the molecules inside have been rearranged and that they are also vibrating a bit more vigorously. They have more energy. When you worked on the block, you transferred energy to it, which is now inside it. By working on the block, you increased its internal energy. The increase in the internal energy is equal to the work done on the block.

The symbol for internal energy is U. The increase in internal energy is given the symbol ΔU:

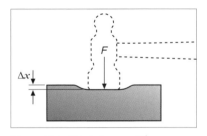

Figure 27.2 *Work done $= F\Delta x$.*

$$\text{increase in internal energy} = \text{work done on the block}$$

$$\Delta U = \Delta W$$

Working electrically on a lead block

- Take a lead block initially at room temperature. Use a low-voltage power supply to drive a current through it for a minute or two (Figure 27.3). Then measure its temperature.
- What has happened to the internal energy of the block?

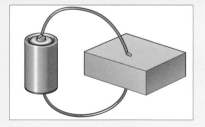

Figure 27.3 *The battery does work on the block.*

Electrical working

If you pass a current through the block of lead, this, too, will transfer energy to the lead. The power supply is applying a force to the electrons inside the lead, and moving them a distance in the direction of the force. As you read in Chapter 1, this is electrical working. It also increases the internal energy of the lead.

Electrical working, like mechanical working, is an ordered process that is not driven by temperature difference. It is quite possible for energy to go from a cold power supply to a hot lead block, or from a low temperature to a high temperature. Again,

increase in internal energy = energy transferred by working

$$\Delta U = \Delta W$$

When a power supply does electrical work,

work done = power × time   or $\Delta W = VI\Delta t$

Heating a lead block

- Leave a lead block to reach room temperature. Measure room temperature. Hold the block in your hands for a few minutes (Figure 27.4). Then measure its temperature.
- What has happened to the internal energy of the block?

Heating

As you know from Chapter 23, you can raise the internal energy of an object by **heating** it. If it is colder than your body temperature, all you need to do is to hold the block closely. You get a bit colder and the block gets a bit hotter. Energy goes from you to the block.

Again, the increase in internal energy of the block is equal to the energy transferred from you to the block. Energy transferred by heating is given the symbol ΔQ. When you heat an object,

increase of internal energy = energy transferred by heating

$$\Delta U = \Delta Q$$

The difference between heating and working

In all three experiments above you transferred energy to the lead block. But the mechanism of transfer was quite different. In the first two situations, the energy was transferred by *working* on the block. In the third situation, it was by *heating*. Heating and working both transfer energy, but in a very important way they are different.

Working is an ordered process that has nothing to do with difference in temperature. It does not matter whether the lead block is hot or cold. You can still work on it by applying a force, and that force moving a distance, or by passing a current through it. Both will increase the internal energy of the lead block. Whatever temperature you are, you can still increase the internal energy of something by working on it.

As you read in Chapter 24, heating is a random process driven by temperature difference. Energy transfer only occurs from you to the object if you are hotter than the object (Figure 27.5). If the object is hotter than you are, the same process transfers energy from the object back to you (Figure 27.6).

Figure 27.4 Hold the block and observe the change in temperature.

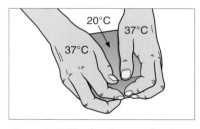

Figure 27.5 You heating an object.

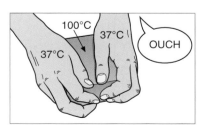

Figure 27.6 The object heating you.

The first law of thermodynamics

The first law of thermodynamics

The **first law of thermodynamics** states that energy is conserved. If you supply energy to a system by working and heating, the internal energy increases by the total amount of energy supplied. You can summarise the first law of thermodynamics by the equation:

$$\frac{\text{increase in}}{\text{internal energy}} = \frac{\text{energy gained}}{\text{by heating}} + \frac{\text{energy gained}}{\text{by working}}$$

$$\Delta U = \Delta Q + \Delta W$$

Here are some examples of this equation in use.

Figure 28.1 *The saucepan and water gain energy by heating from the flame so ΔQ is positive. No work is being done so $\Delta W = 0$. The increase in internal energy is equal to the energy gained by heating $\Delta U = \Delta Q$.*

Figure 28.2 *The power drill works on the wall and twist drill and so ΔW is positive. The wall and the twist drill get hotter and so ΔU is positive. Some energy is lost by heating to the surroundings and so ΔQ is negative.*

$$\frac{\text{Internal energy}}{\text{gained by the}} = \frac{\text{work done}}{\text{by the power}} - \frac{\text{energy lost}}{\text{by heating}}$$
twist drill and   drill and wall   to the room.
wall

$$\Delta U = \Delta W - \Delta Q.$$

Figure 28.3 *The wire in the bunsen flame is red hot. Its temperature is constant and so its internal energy is constant and $\Delta U = 0$. No work is being done, so $\Delta W = 0$. The wire gains energy (by heating) from the flame. This is a positive term $\Delta Q_{flame\ to\ wire}$. The wire loses energy by heating to the room. This is an equal and opposite term $\Delta Q_{wire\ to\ room}$.*
$$\Delta Q_{flame\ to\ wire} = -\Delta Q_{wire\ to\ room}.$$
The net gain of energy is zero:
$$\Delta Q_{flame\ to\ wire} + \Delta Q_{wire\ to\ room} = 0.$$

Insulated situations

If the vacuum flasks in Figure 28.4 are good insulators, it does not matter whether their contents are hot or cold – they are thermally isolated. They neither gain nor lose energy by heating.

If you apply the equation $\Delta U = \Delta Q + \Delta W$ to the contents, the energy transferred by heating, ΔQ, is zero. Therefore $\Delta U = \Delta W$.

If a system is at the same temperature as its surroundings, no heating takes place anyway, so again ΔQ is zero and $\Delta U = \Delta W$.

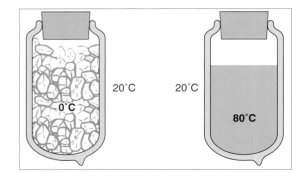

Figure 28.4 *The flasks are isolated. Their contents neither gain energy from nor lose energy to their surroundings.*

Complete isolation

There is no work being done either electrically or mechanically on or by the flasks in Figure 28.4. So ΔW is zero as well as ΔQ. If you apply the equation $\Delta U = \Delta Q + \Delta W$, you can see that ΔU is zero – there is no change in internal energy. The internal energy is constant.

The contents of the flasks are completely isolated from their surroundings, and so their internal energy is constant.

There are very few systems that are completely isolated from their surroundings. Bodies in space, like the Sun, are continuously losing energy by giving out heat. The Earth in space has roughly a constant temperature and constant internal energy because it is gaining energy from the Sun and also radiating an equal amount into space.

Perhaps the only really isolated system is the universe as a whole, which, so far as we are aware, is neither gaining energy from nor losing energy to anywhere else (Figure 28.5).

Figure 28.5 The internal energy of the universe is probably constant. It makes you wonder where the energy came from in the first place.

WORKED EXAMPLE

A 100 W filament lamp takes 200 ms to reach full brightness. Show how the equation $\Delta U = \Delta Q + \Delta W$ may be applied to the filament (a) during the first 0.001 ms after it is switched on and (b) after it has been switched on for some time.

(a) The filament takes 200 ms to reach full brightness. So in 0.001 ms, the temperature rises a little, but insufficient to heat its surroundings. During this time the power supply is working on the filament because a current is flowing through the filament. So ΔW is positive. The filament is still very nearly at the same temperature as its surroundings. So no heating is going on: ΔQ is zero. The work done by the power supply is used to raise the internal energy. $\Delta U = \Delta W$, and ΔQ is zero. Figure 28.6 summarises this situation.

(b) After the lamp has been switched on for some time, it has reached a steady operating temperature. If its temperature is steady, its internal energy is not changing. So ΔU is zero. Since $\Delta U = \Delta Q + \Delta W$, then $0 = \Delta Q + \Delta W$. Again, ΔW is positive: the power supply is still working on the filament. This means that ΔQ must be negative. So the energy gained by the filament by heating is negative: the filament is losing energy by heating. The filament is now heating the surroundings because, at its operating temperature, it is now hotter than the surroundings. Figure 28.7 summarises this situation.

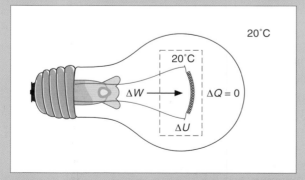

Figure 28.6 When the filament is at room temperature, all the work done by the power supply increases its internal energy:
$\Delta U = \Delta W.$

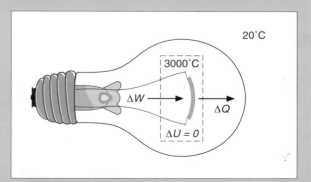

Figure 28.7 When the filament is at operating temperature, the work done by the power supply is equal to the energy lost by the filament heating the room: $\Delta Q = -\Delta W.$

Heat engines and heat pumps

Thermal power stations

If you want to power a vacuum cleaner, a motor vehicle, or an industrial machine, you want to use your primary energy sources, such as coal, gas and oil, to do work.

A **heat engine** is a device that will take energy from a hot body and use it to do work. All thermal power stations – power stations that produce steam to drive turbines – make use of heat engines.

Figure 29.1 shows a block diagram of a thermal power station. The boiler, heated by gas, oil, coal or nuclear fuel, produces steam at high pressure. The steam passes through the turbine, forcing the blades to rotate, which turns the generator, producing electricity.

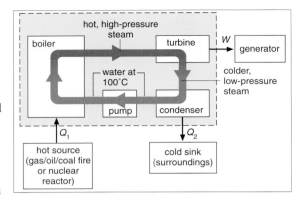

Figure 29.1 The power station uses a temperature difference to do work.

Turbines are designed to use as much energy as possible from hot, high-pressure steam. But they still give out waste low-pressure steam that is still quite hot. That steam is taken to a condenser, which turns it back into water, giving out latent heat. This waste energy is given out to the atmosphere. The liquid water is then pumped back into the boiler to be turned to high-pressure steam again.

There are three important energy flows in a power station. The first is Q_1, the energy taken by heating from the hot source, which heats the boiler. The second is W, the work done by the turbine on the generator. The third is Q_2, the energy given by heating from the condenser to the cool atmosphere.

Another common heat engine is the internal combustion engine, but there are others, for instance the thermocouple in Figure 29.2.

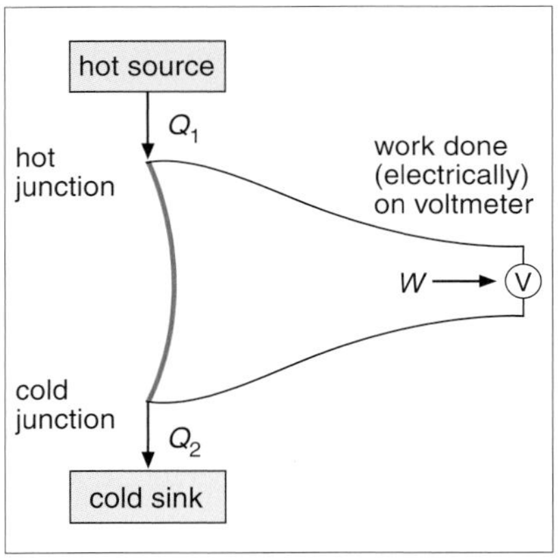

All heat engines take energy from a hot source. They cannot use all of this to do work, only a part. The rest of the energy they give out by heating to something cold, called a cold sink.

Figure 29.2 The thermocouple uses a temperature difference to do work.

Efficiency

When you walk about or run upstairs, you do work. To do this work you need energy released as your food combines with oxygen from the air. The energy you need is always more than the work you do. No energy is lost; you don't put out less energy than you take in. It is just that you don't use all the energy you take in to do work moving about or raising yourself up.

This is true for almost any process that any machine, engine or mechanical device undertakes. The useful output is never greater than the input, and it is almost always less than the input. For efficient devices, less of the input is wasted and a bigger proportion is useful output.

We define **efficiency** as the proportion of the work or energy input that comes out usefully:

$$\text{efficiency} = \frac{\text{useful output}}{\text{input}}$$

The efficiency of systems varies over a wide range. A manual car gear box is well over 95 per cent efficient; a car engine is less than 40 per cent efficient.

Efficiency of a heat engine

Applying the law of conservation of energy to the heat engine (Figure 29.3), we get:

energy from hot source = work done + energy given to cold sink
$$Q_1 = W + Q_2$$

which can be rewritten as

$$W = Q_1 - Q_2$$

The efficiency of a heat engine is the ratio of W, the work done by the engine, to Q_1, the energy taken by heating from the high-temperature source. So

$$\text{efficiency} = \frac{W}{Q_1} = \frac{(Q_1 - Q_2)}{Q_1} = 1 - \frac{Q_2}{Q_1}$$

There is always some energy flow to the cold sink; Q_2 cannot be zero. So a heat engine can never be 100% efficient.

Theoretical efficiency of a heat engine

It can be shown that the maximum efficiency of a heat engine depends on the Kelvin temperatures T_1 of the hot source and T_2 of the cold sink (Figure 29.4):

$$\textbf{maximum efficiency} = 1 - \frac{T_2}{T_1}$$

Only if the temperature of the sink T_2 is 0 K could the efficiency be as high as 100%. For thermal power stations, the sink temperature has a minimum of 373 K (= 100°C, the boiling point of water). Turbine designers are constantly looking for higher-temperature materials so that they can raise the source temperature to increase the efficiency.

Today's turbines operate at about 600°C (873 K). So for them

$$\textbf{maximum efficiency} = 1 - \frac{T_2}{T_1} = 1 - \frac{373}{873} = 57\%$$

In practice, efficiencies are about 40%.

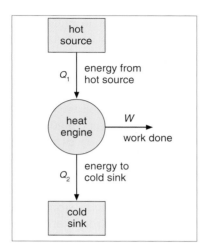

Figure 29.3 Heat input from hot source = work done by engine + heat given to cold sink.

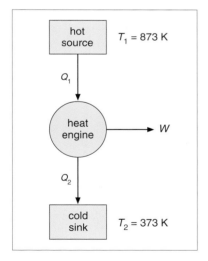

Figure 29.4 Efficiency of a heat engine = $1 - T_2/T_1$.

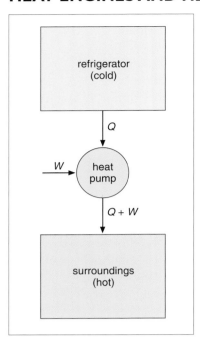

Figure 29.5 A heat pump pumps internal energy out of the refrigerator into the hotter surroundings.

Heat pumps

If you put a hot body next to a cold body, energy flows from hot to cold. If you connect a heat engine between a hot and a cold body, the engine uses the temperature difference to do work.

Internal energy flows naturally from hot to cold. A **heat pump** can pump energy from cold to hot. It works the opposite way round from a heat engine. Mechanical work W is done on it; it takes energy Q from the cold body and gives energy $Q + W$ to the hot body (Figure 29.5). Refrigerators, freezers and air conditioners use heat pumps to pump internal energy from cold to hot.

Energy spreading around

When something is oscillating, for instance a swinging pendulum or a mass oscillating on a spring, that oscillater is subject to resistive forces and gradually leaks energy to its surroundings. The friction acting on moving surfaces and between the oscillator and the air transfers energy to the surroundings. If this energy is not replaced, the oscillations eventually stop.

At the beginning, the oscillator was a relatively concentrated energy store. At the end, the energy has been spread around and has increased the internal energy of the surroundings. You know that the same thing happens when a hot body is in contact with cold surroundings.

The natural tendency is for all concentrated stores of energy to become spread out. Our primary energy stores become smaller: the energy they have is dissipated as internal energy. In our universe, the stars become colder and the temperature differences are reduced. The universe's temperature differences do work. They are even the power sources for life. So as the fires of the universe die out, so will life, if things get that far!

Astrophysics

It is difficult to look at the night sky without a sense of how marvellous it is. The philosopher Immanuel Kant (1724–1804) said, 'Two things fill the mind with ever-increasing wonder and awe, the more often and the more intensely the mind of thought is drawn to them: the starry heavens above me and the moral law within me'. From quite a different perspective, the writer of the psalms said, 'When I consider your heavens, the work of your fingers, the Moon and the stars, which you have set in place, what is man that you care for him?'

Our own eyes tell us of the vastness of the universe. The more we look at the sky, the more stars we can see. And we can sense the huge distances between the stars, which remind us how small we are. This option gives us an opportunity to find out more about the universe in which we live.

Observing stars

The first astronomers used their naked eyes. Next came telescopes to help the eye. But now, astronomers rarely look at the stars directly. They make most observations of stars by taking photographs (Figure A1). More recently, they have used electronic charge coupled devices (CCDs) (Figure A2) to record images. These give out an electrical signal which depends on the light they receive.

Our eyes have limits to how clearly they can observe. The retina at the back of the eye has many small light-detecting cells. The size of these cells determines how well we can see. Cells with a large surface area can use this area to collect a lot of light, so they would be able to detect very dim objects. But they would not be able to detect very precisely which part of the retina the light was hitting, so the image would be unclear. Small cells would locate the light precisely, but would not be very sensitive.

The same is true with photographic film and CCDs. Photographic film has grains of light-sensitive chemical. Film with large grains is sensitive to light, but produces a very 'grainy' image (Figure A3). Film with small grains is less sensitive, but produces a sharper image (Figure A4).

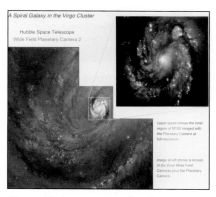

Figure A1 Astronomers often look at photographs instead of observing the sky directly.

Figure A2 Charge coupled device: like television cameras and astronomical telescopes, astronomers often use Charge Coupled Devices to record images.

Figure A3 If the grain of the film is large, the film is sensitive, but the image is grainy.

Figure A4 This is the same scene as Figure A3, but the grain of the film is much smaller.

ASTROPHYSICS

Figure A5 The array of a CCD: the array on this CCD is 800 × 800 pixels.

CCDs have arrays (many regular lines) of sensitive pixels (picture cells). For clarity, the astronomer wants very small pixels, but such CCDs are not very sensitive (Figure A5).

Our eyes have a good balance between sensitivity and clarity. In a similar way, astronomers have to balance the need for sensitivity (requiring large detecting areas) with the need for clarity (requiring small detecting areas).

Efficiency and linearity

Astronomers want both their film and their CCDs to be efficient, so that they detect very small amounts of light. But they also want to detect the difference between different levels of light. With a CCD, they want a small signal from a dim light, and a large signal from a bright light. They want the CCD to be linear, so that the output signal is proportional to the light received.

Your eyes have a limited range of frequencies to which they are sensitive. The same is true for CCDs and so the efficiency and linearity of CCDs vary with frequency and astronomers tailor their CCDs to the frequencies they are observing.

The effect of the atmosphere

Figure A6 The Hubble Space Telescope seen from the Space Shuttle.

All visual observations on the Earth's surface rely on light that has passed through the Earth's atmosphere. And the atmosphere has an effect upon the light. Changes in atmospheric density cause stars to twinkle. The air and dust in it absorb and scatter more than 30% of the visible light incident on the Earth. Different wavelengths are absorbed by differing amounts, distorting the information we receive.

If you want to avoid this absorption and scattering, you need a telescope in orbit above the Earth's atmosphere.

The Infrared Astronomical Satellite (IRAS) went into orbit in 1983. It created a detailed far-infra-red map of our view of the universe. In the early 1990s, the Cosmic Background Explorer (COBE) detected small ripples in the microwave background radiation reaching the Earth. The Hubble Space Telescope (Figure A6) continues to produce some stunning pictures (Figure A7).

How far away are the stars?

Figure A7 The Cygnus Loop supernova remnant, as seen from the Hubble Space Telescope.

Astronomical distances are so great that special units are used. Two of these are shown in Table A1.

Table A.1 *Two units used for astronomical distances*

Unit	Definition	Metre equivalent
Astronomical Unit (AU)	Average distance between Earth and Sun	1 AU = 1.496×10^{11} m
Light year (ly)	Distance travelled by light in one year	1 ly = 9.46×10^{15} m

The distance to a nearby star is measured using trigonometric parallax. Figure A8 shows how this is done. Figure A8a shows two stars viewed from the Earth at times 6 months apart. In July the angle measured between the stars is θ. In January there is a smaller angle α; the nearby star seems to be closer to the distant star. Figure A8b shows the position of the nearby star compared with the position of a very distant star. The parallax angle $\left(\dfrac{\theta - \alpha}{2}\right)$ (Figure A8b) is

measured and $\tan\left(\dfrac{\theta - \alpha}{2}\right) = \dfrac{1\ \text{AU}}{D} \quad \therefore D = \dfrac{1\ \text{AU}}{\tan\left(\dfrac{\theta - \alpha}{2}\right)}$

Even the closest star is very far away, and the angle $\dfrac{\theta - \alpha}{2}$ is extremely small.

This angle gets even smaller for more distant stars. Parallax angles down to $1/360000°$ can be measured, making this method suitable for measuring star distances up to 10^{18} m – about 100 light years.

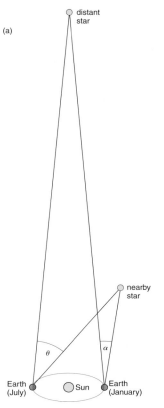

nearby star

Earth (July) Sun Earth (January)

Figure A8(a) As the Earth moves round the Sun, the position of the nearby star moves relative to the more distant star.

The energy distribution from a star

The radiation given out by a star has a range of wavelengths. Figure A9 shows the energy distribution. Look at the graph for the star at 1000 K. It gives out radiation with wavelengths from 1 μm to longer than 5 μm. But the graph has a

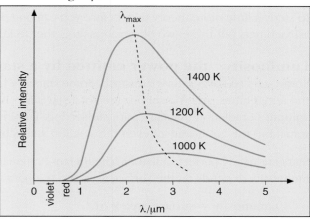

Figure A9 Energy distribution for stars at different temperatures.

peak at about 3 μm, showing that the radiation is strongest at this wavelength. The wavelength at which the emitted radiation is strongest, is called λ_{max}.

Wien's law

If you heat a piece of steel wire, it first becomes red hot. As it gets hotter, it emits a wider range of visible light and becomes white hot. If you look again at Figure A9, you can see why this happens. As you look from the graph for 1000 K to the graphs for 1200 K and 1400 K, you can see that the wavelength at which the graph peaks, λ_{max}, gets shorter. The hotter the body, the shorter λ_{max}.

For a star, there is a simple connection between temperature and λ_{max}, called Wien's law, that states:

λ_{max} is inversely proportional to the Kelvin temperature T

$\lambda_{max} \propto \dfrac{1}{T}$

So $\lambda_{max} = \dfrac{\text{constant}}{T}$. This constant has the value 2.898×10^{-3} m K.

The values of λ_{max} on Figure A9 lie in the infra-red, although the body at 1400 K emits a small amount of visible light and appears 'red hot'.

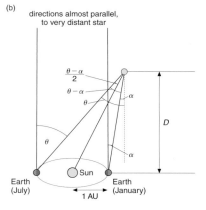

Figure A8(b)

$tan\left(\dfrac{\theta - \alpha}{2}\right) = \dfrac{1\ AU}{D}$

$\therefore D = \dfrac{1\ AU}{tan\left(\dfrac{\theta - \alpha}{2}\right)}.$

Astronomical objects whose intensity peaks at X-ray wavelengths are at extremely high temperatures (10^7 K), whereas those peaking at radio wavelengths are close to absolute zero.

Wien's law enables astronomers to measure the surface temperature of any distant star, simply by measuring λ_{max}. You can do this yourself by observation and looking for those stars in the sky which are reddish in colour, and therefore relatively cold, and those which are bluish and therefore relatively hot.

Observation shows the Sun to be yellow-red, so its λ_{max} is about 500 nm. Use Wien's law to calculate its surface temperature.

Finding out more about stars

From what you have read above, you can see that for any star, astronomers can measure its temperature by observations from the Earth. And they can measure the distance away of stars that are less than about 100 light years away. You need to study a little more theory first, before you can understand exactly how astronomers put these two observations together to learn about stars.

Luminosity: the power emitted by a star

Some stars are large: some are small. Some stars are hot: some are cold. Both the temperature and the surface area of a star affect its luminosity – the total amount of radiation the star emits per second. Luminosity is measured in watts, but the luminosity of even the smallest star is billions of watts.

Stars are nearly perfect radiators. The Stefan–Boltzman law describes how luminosity depends on the surface area and temperature of a star:

$$\text{Luminosity} = \text{surface area} \times \sigma T^4$$

where T is the surface temperature of the star and σ is a constant called 'Stefan's constant'.

Stefan's constant has the value 5.67×10^{-8} W m^{-2} K^{-4}.

Stars are roughly spherical, so their surface area is equal to $4\pi r^2$ where r is the star's radius. This gives the formula:

$$\text{Luminosity} = 4\pi r^2 \sigma T^4$$

The radius of the Sun is about 7×10^8 m. The surface temperature of the Sun is about 5800 K. Use this information with Stefan's law to find the luminosity of the Sun.

Luminosity is often expressed in terms of the luminosity of the Sun. For example, a star of luminosity $6 \times 10^{-4} L_\odot$ has 6×10^{-4} of the luminosity of the Sun.

Intensity

The power radiated by a star travels in all directions. Only a tiny amount of it reaches the Earth. Think about two stars with the same luminosity. They both give out the same power. But if one of the stars is closer to Earth than the other, more of its power will reach the Earth. The intensity of a star is the power per metre squared from it that arrives on the Earth. A distant star has less intensity than a close star of the same luminosity. And a star of higher luminosity has a greater intensity than a star of lower luminosity the same distance away.

Intensity depends on luminosity L and also on distance D away from the Earth by the formula:

$$\text{Intensity} = \frac{L}{4\pi D^2}$$

Astronomers use their telescopes to measure the intensity of any star. And you know that they can use parallax to measure D, the distance away, of many close stars. Using the formula above, astronomers therefore can calculate the luminosity of stars close to the Earth.

Temperature: the Hertzsprung–Russell diagram

Astronomers can find the temperature of a star from the wavelength of maximum intensity, using Wien's law. From measurements of intensity and distance, they can also calculate the luminosity of close stars. After doing this, they plot luminosity against decreasing temperature of all the close stars. Figure A10 shows the graph they obtain. It is called the Hertzsprung–Russell (H–R) diagram. The original versions of this diagram labelled the horizontal axis in terms of the *type* of light the star emitted. This corresponds to temperature decreasing to the right.

The star plots on the H–R diagram form a distinct pattern, a curve from top left to bottom right through the centre of the diagram. This pattern involves a wide variety of stars: from extremely massive, luminous blue stars (top left) to extremely dim and less-massive red stars (bottom right).

This curved line, which shows the relationship between luminosity and temperature for many stars, is called the *main sequence*. This confusing name implies that stars move along it in order. In fact, stars *stay at the same point* on the main sequence for most of their lives.

Figure A10 also shows two groups of stars above and towards the right of the main sequence. These are cool (red) stars with a high luminosity. For low-temperature stars to emit this much power, they must have a very large surface area. Hence, they are known as *red giants* and *red supergiants*.

Another group of stars is shown below and towards the left of the main sequence. These are hot (white) stars with a low luminosity. For high-temperature stars to emit so little power, they must have a very small surface area. Hence, they are known as *white dwarfs*.

All these groups consist of stars that have completed their core-hydrogen fusion and left the main sequence. You will find more about these later in this Option.

Measuring distances to more distant stars

Astronomers can use parallax to find the distance of close stars, only. For distant stars, they use the H–R diagram. First, they measure the temperature, as for any star, using Wien's law. Then they use the H–R diagram to predict the luminosity L. Finally, they measure the intensity. Then, they use the formula

Intensity $= \dfrac{L}{4\pi D^2}$, to calculate the distance D.

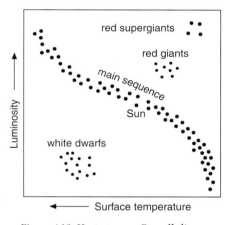

Figure A10 Hertzsprung–Russell diagram.

ASTROPHYSICS

Cepheid variables

There is a type of star called a *Cepheid variable*. The brightness of these stars varies with a period that depends on their luminosity. If astronomers measure the period of a distant Cepheid variable, they can find the luminosity and hence can calculate the distance from the Earth. There are Cepheid variables in many galaxies, which enable astronomers to calculate the distances of these galaxies from Earth.

The lives of stars

Many of us wish to understand how the universe around us came into being. Human beings were not around to observe the beginnings of the first stars, so astrophysicists use observations of the universe around us to suggest theories of how the stars came into being.

The most abundant element in the stars around us is hydrogen. The most plausible theory is that stars begin as clouds of hydrogen. Gravitational forces between the hydrogen atoms pull them together and so the cloud collapses under its own gravitational forces. As the atoms get closer, their gravitational potential energy decreases and their kinetic energy increases. You saw in Chapter 22 that temperature is proportional to the mean kinetic energy of the atoms. So you can see that the temperature of the hydrogen gas increases as the atoms get closer.

If the cloud's mass is large, the temperature increases enormously. When the cloud's mass is at least 100 times that of our Sun, this high temperature causes the hydrogen atoms to bang into each other so hard that some of them stick together. They fuse together to make helium. Astrophysicists call this *burning* hydrogen.

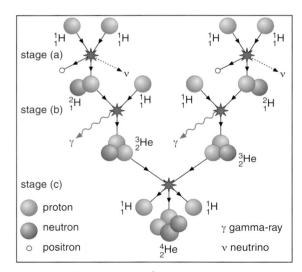

Figure A11 Proton–proton chain.

Energy from fusion

When hydrogen fuses to form helium, energy is released. This process is called the proton–proton chain. Figure A11 shows the *p–p chain* in detail. It involves the emission of neutrinos as the protons combine.

The p-p chain consists of three stages:

(a) $\quad {}_1^1\text{H} + {}_1^1\text{H} \rightarrow {}_1^2\text{H} + {}_1^0\beta^+ + \nu$

(b) $\quad {}_1^2\text{H} + {}_1^1\text{H} \rightarrow {}_2^3\text{He} + \gamma$

(c) $\quad {}_2^3\text{He} + {}_2^3\text{He} \rightarrow {}_2^4\text{He} + 2{}_1^1\text{H}$

The whole fusion reaction can be represented by the equation:

4 protons $\Rightarrow$ helium nucleus + energy

Nuclear masses are measured in *unified mass units*, u. During the fusion of hydrogen to make helium, when each helium nucleus is formed, four protons, of total mass 4.01996 u become a helium nucleus of mass 4.00255 u. The difference in mass is 0.017 u, which is 4.36746×10^{-29} kg. This is the mass of the energy released.

$$\text{Mass of 4 protons} = \text{mass of helium nucleus} + \text{mass of energy released}$$

$$4.01996 \text{ u} = 4.00255 \text{ u} + 0.017 \text{ u}$$

The mass of the energy emitted is 0.017 u, or 4.36746×10^{-29} kg.

If you want to start fusion on Earth, you need much higher temperatures than in a star. Because stars are so big, there are many protons available. Only a few of them need to be going fast enough to fuse. A comparatively small fusion reactor on Earth would need much higher temperatures to get fusion going.

You can calculate the amount of energy released using Einstein's equation $E = mc^2$, where E is the energy released, m is the mass of that energy and c is the speed of light.

For the fusion of four protons to a helium nucleus, the amount of energy released is

$$E = 4.36746 \times 10^{-29} \text{ kg} \times (3.0 \times 10^8 \text{ m s}^{-1})^2 = 3.93 \times 10^{-12} \text{ J}.$$

This is a vast amount of energy for four tiny protons. In every star, there is a large number of individual fusion reactions occurring every second. For instance, the Sun has a luminosity of 3.8×10^{26} W. You can use this figure to calculate the enormous number of individual fusion reactions taking place per second.

Life on the main sequence

The energy released by fusion gives kinetic energy to particles in a star, enabling them to move away from the star's centre and causing the star to expand. At the same time, gravity pulls the particles together. For most of a star's life, these two effects are balanced, and the star keeps a fairly constant size during a long period of burning hydrogen. Stars on the main sequence are in this condition.

Larger stars have larger gravitational forces. This pulls them in harder. They reach higher temperatures, burn faster, and have higher luminosity. These are stars towards the top left of the H–R diagram in Figure A10. Large stars have shorter lives than small stars because they are faster burning and so they spend less time on the main sequence.

Smaller stars have lower gravitational forces. Their temperatures, needed to balance the gravitational forces, and their corresponding luminosities are lower than for big stars, but they have longer lives. They are at the bottom right of the H–R diagram in Figure A10.

ASTROPHYSICS

White dwarfs

Stars less than 0.4 times the mass of the Sun burn the hydrogen very slowly for a long time. Eventually, when the hydrogen is used up, gravity causes these stars to contract further. They become *white dwarfs*, at the bottom end of the H–R diagram. White dwarfs are extremely dense – a hundred tons per teaspoonful. Gravitational forces pull them strongly together but electron degeneracy, the fact that all electrons must have their separate spaces, keeps them from collapsing. There are no nuclear reactions releasing energy in white dwarfs but their density and initial high temperature gives them enough internal energy to give out light for hundreds of millions of years.

Red giants

Stars between 0.4 and 8 times the mass of the Sun become *red giants* (Figure A12) at the end of their lives. Nuclear processes in the core of a main-sequence star stop once there is insufficient hydrogen there for fusion. The core temperature is too low for fusion of helium nuclei to occur immediately. An envelope of unburned hydrogen remains outside the core.

As fusion stops in the core, gravitational forces again become dominant and the core contracts, causing the star's temperature to increase. Fusion of the hydrogen now occurs in a shell around the core. The region of fusion is now further out, and so there is less matter outside it to squash it in. There is sufficient energy released to cause the outer envelope of the star to expand, while the shell continues to fuse. The star's diameter increases by a factor of about 100 during this stage of the process. The star cools and becomes red due to the lower temperature (Wien's law), forming a red giant.

Figure A12 A red giant.

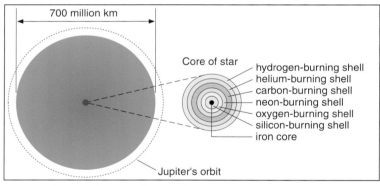

Figure A13 Fusion layers within a red supergiant.

The more massive the star, the greater its ultimate core temperature. The core temperature may reach a point where helium fusion occurs, leading to the formation of beryllium and carbon. These reactions release energy and raise the temperature of the core.

As the core continues to fuse, the temperature continues to increase. This causes larger nuclei to fuse and create even heavier elements. This process takes place progressively, in shells. So as one fusion process ends, the next process begins, but only when the star has heated up even more. The most massive stars are capable of forming an iron core surrounded by layers supporting different fusion processes, as shown in Figure A13.

Large amounts of matter are ejected from the distant outer envelope of a red giant where the gravitational field is weaker. A red giant loses mass ten million times faster than the Sun.

At some point, the energy available from further gravitational collapse is insufficient to trigger the next fusion stage. The layers outside the core continue fusion for some time. The inactive core region grows. For stars between 0.4 and 8 solar masses, the fire effectively goes out and gravitational forces finally succeed in collapsing the star. The core remnant of the red giant

70

cools down and shrinks. As it contracts, its gravitational potential energy decreases and the star becomes very hot. Like the stars with a small mass, these finally become white dwarfs.

Supernovae

Stars with original masses greater than eight times that of the Sun also become giant stars – in this case, supergiants. If the Sun became a red supergiant, it would engulf almost all the space out to the orbit of Jupiter. The destruction of supergiants is spectacular! Because of their enormous mass, they collapse more. Their atoms are squeezed so much that electrons in the core combine with protons to form neutrons and the core collapses very rapidly. A large amount of energy is released and blows away the star's outer layers into interstellar space. The resulting shock wave heats up the dispersing gas and forms a very bright supernova (Figure A14).

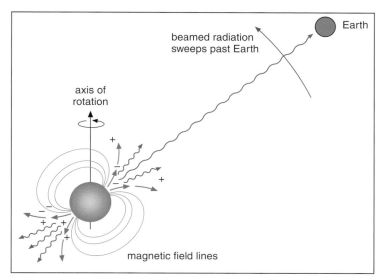

Figure A14 A supernova (circled in yellow) in the spiral galaxy M99.

Neutron stars

If the core remnant after a supernova is more than about 1.4 solar masses the gravitational forces are strong enough to overcome the electron degeneracy and collapse the protons and electrons to form neutrons. These neutron stars are extremely dense objects. They are like a giant nucleus. Typically, they will contain a mass of about 10^{30} kg, within a diameter of 20 km, giving a density about 10^{15} times greater than normal matter – a million tons in a pinhead.

With such small surface areas, neutron stars emit insufficient thermal radiation for detection by normal visual or thermal telescopes. However, since they are both magnetised and rotating, they continually emit a high-frequency radio signal along their magnetic axis (Figure A15).

Figure A15 Rotating neutron stars produce pulsars.

This signal sweeps across space as the neutron star rotates, in a similar way to the beam of light issuing from a lighthouse. A pulse of radio waves is detected each time the beam sweeps past the Earth. *Pulsars* were first detected in 1967. Their connection with neutron stars and supernovae was established a year later when a pulsar was found at the centre of the Crab nebula (Figure A16). The supernova which formed this was recorded by Chinese astronomers in 1054.

Figure A16 The Crab nebula has a pulsar at its centre.

Black holes

If the neutron core is greater than about 2.5 solar masses, gravitational attraction is strong enough to shrink the core until it is no more than a point, referred to as a *singularity*. A black hole is a region of space, surrounding a singularity, from within which no light, matter or signal of any kind can achieve the required velocity to escape. Despite this, detection is still possible where a black hole is part of a binary system. Material sucked from the companion star becomes extremely hot and emits X-rays as it falls into the black hole. Strong X-ray sources, associated with a single star, indicate the presence of a companion black hole.

Solid Materials

For thousands of years, people have made amazing and beautiful structures. Yet even as recently as two hundred years ago, engineers knew almost nothing about the properties of the solid materials they were working with. These people did not use the principles of physics that you will learn here, such as proportionality and elasticity. They simply followed the examples of others' work and relied on their own instinctive 'feel' for solid materials. Today, all engineers are expected to know much more. And the basic principles presented here are the starting point.

Tension and extension

Stretching springs

Hang a spring from a clamp stand and fix a rule with its zero at the lower end of the spring.

In 0.5 newton steps, add weights to the spring (Figure S1), measuring the extension for each.

Every 3 N, unload again completely in steps of 0.5 N and then reload, again in steps of 0.5 N. Measure the extension every time you change the tension. Plot a graph of tension against extension.

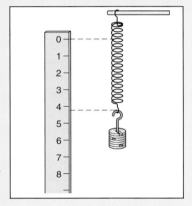

Figure S1 Each weight added extends the spring.

Proportionality

The first part of the tension–extension graph for a spring is a straight line. Robert Hooke produced a law about the behaviour of materials. When applied to springs, **Hooke's law** states:

> up to a limit, the extension of a spring is proportional to the tension
>
> tension ∝ extension

which can be written in symbols as: $F \propto x$ or $F = kx$, where k is a constant called the spring constant.

Spring constant: If tension is measured in newtons (N) and extension in metres (m), then k has units of newtons per metre (N m^{-1}). You can think of the spring constant as a measure of the stiffness of the spring. A stiff spring has a larger spring constant than a flexible spring; the stiff spring needs a larger tension than the flexible spring for a given extension.

The graph illustrated in Figure S2 has a spring constant of 50 N m⁻¹: in other words, the spring would need 50 N to extend it 1 m (if you could extend it that far)!

Elasticity

Elastic limit: If you apply a small tension to a spring and then remove that tension, the spring returns to its original length. This will happen up to a limit, called the *elastic limit*.

Limit of proportionality: Above a certain tension, the spring graph is no longer a straight line; the extension is no longer proportional to the tension. The point above which this happens is called the *limit of proportionality*, or sometimes the *Hooke's law limit*.

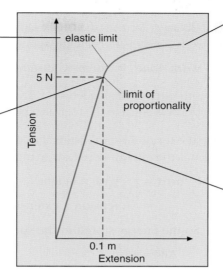

Figure S2 Graph shows a spring constant of 50 N m⁻¹ – it would take 50N to extend the spring one metre.

Above the elastic limit, the spring's behaviour is *plastic* (it deforms permanently). When you remove the tension, the extension does not return to zero. You cannot find the elastic limit by looking at a graph – only by experimenting to find the smallest tension that produces a permanent extension.

Below the elastic limit, the spring is elastic; extensions of the spring are not permanent. When you remove the tension, the extension returns to zero.

You can see from these definitions that the elastic limit and the limit of proportionality are quite different in meaning; but for a spring, the two limits are very close together. Figure S2 shows that the elastic limit occurs just after the limit of proportionality.

Measuring energy stored in a spring

Hold a 100 g mass hanger with the hook just above the bottom loop of the spring (Figure S3). Release the mass hanger and measure the maximum extension of the spring when the mass hanger reaches the bottom of its travel.

Calculate the potential energy lost by the mass hanger falling. What is the kinetic energy of the mass and spring at the bottom of the fall? What energy is stored in the spring?

Repeat, increasing the falling mass in 100 g steps.

Plot a graph of energy stored in the spring against extension. What relationship do you observe?

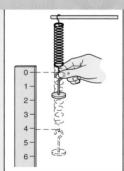

Figure S3 When you release the mass hanger, the spring extends.

Energy stored in a spring

If you stretch a spring elastically, the energy stored in the spring is equal to the work done stretching it. Figure S4 shows the proportional part of a tension–extension graph for a spring. The shaded area is where the spring is extended by a small distance, Δx, (Δ is the Greek capital letter 'delta'. It means a small change.) The work done in stretching the spring a distance Δx with a force F is given by:

$$\text{work done } = \text{ force } \times \text{ distance } = F\,\Delta x$$

This is the area of the shaded strip. The total work done in stretching from zero to extension x is equal to the total area between the graph and the extension axis.

Since the tension is proportional to the extension, the area under the graph (which is the energy stored), is triangular. The area is given by:

$$\text{area} = \tfrac{1}{2} \times \text{base} \times \text{height}$$
$$= \tfrac{1}{2} \times \text{tension} \times \text{extension}$$

So the energy stored in the spring is:

$$\Delta W = \tfrac{1}{2}Fx$$

Since $F = kx$, we get

$$\Delta W = \tfrac{1}{2}(kx)x = \tfrac{1}{2}kx^2$$

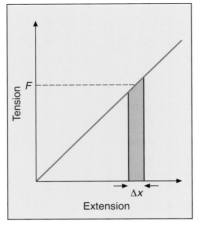

Figure S4 The energy stored in a spring is equal to the work done stretching it.

Stretching copper

EYE PROTECTION MUST BE WORN

Take a long length of thin copper wire and fasten it to a long bench as shown in Figure S5.
Measure the extension of the wire for a range of tensions.
Unload and reload, measuring the tensions and extensions part-way through your experiment.
Plot a graph of tension against extension.

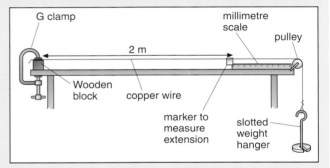

Figure S5 Attach copper wire to the bench and measure its extension for a range of tensions.

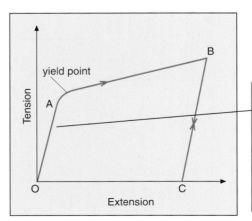

Figure S6 Tension–extension graph for copper.

The behaviour of copper

The tension-extension graph for copper (Figure S6) is a straight line where the extension is small, showing that extension is proportional to tension.

The copper is elastic in this region – the extension returns to zero if the force (tension) is removed. In this region of the graph, forces applied to the copper slightly increase the *distance* between its atoms without changing the *positions* of the atoms. The forces stretch the atomic bonds without breaking them. This elastic behaviour does *not* absorb energy – the work done on the copper when you stretch it is equal to the work done by the copper when it is released. The elastic limit of the wire is called the *yield point* (see 'Yielding', later in this Option).

If you stretch copper past the linear region, it deforms permanently. Some of the atoms slide over each other: this is called *plastic flow*. Plastic flow occurs after the yield point. Forces that take the copper above the yield point break bonds between atoms in the copper and rearrange them. When you remove the force, the atoms are unable to return to their original positions. Plastic deformation absorbs energy. Some energy is used to break bonds, some is used to increase the temperature of the copper as the atoms slide over each other.

This area represents the energy needed to stretch a copper wire *elastically*.

This area represents the energy used to stretch the copper wire *plastically*, to breaking. It is much greater.

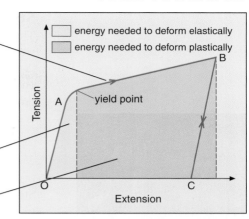

Figure S7 *The energy needed to stretch the copper wire elastically is less than the energy needed to stretch it plastically.*

Pre-stretched copper

If you unload and reload a copper wire after it has undergone some plastic flow, the graph is a straight line (BC) parallel to the first loading line (line OA in Figures S6 and S7). If you are given a piece of pre-stretched copper wire to test, you would get a graph like that in Figure S8. You can see that Figure S8 is merely the final parts of Figures S6 and S7 moved back to the origin.

Copper wire straight from the reel is tough. It can absorb large amounts of energy by plastic deformation, so it needs a lot of energy to break it. Pre-stretched copper wire is brittle. It cannot absorb energy by plastic deformation, so needs little energy to break it.

Mild steel (as used in car bodies) is tough and can absorb much of the energy involved in a car crash. So, less energy is available to damage the passengers.

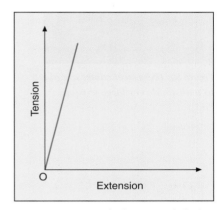

Figure S8 *Pre-stretched wire needs little energy to break it.*

Stress, strain and the Young modulus

Breaking strands

Measure the diameter of a thin copper wire, and then the force needed to break it.

Repeat with copper wire in a range of different thicknesses.

Predict the relationship between the force needed to break a wire and its cross-sectional area.

Plot a graph to check your prediction.

Stress and strain

The strength of a wire depends on its cross-sectional area. Thick wires are stronger than thin wires of the same material.

For a given material, the tension needed to break the wire divided by the cross-sectional area is constant. The tension divided by cross-sectional area is called the *tensile stress*, σ, (the small Greek letter 'sigma'):

$$\text{tensile stress} = \frac{\text{tension}}{\text{cross-sectional area}}$$

Stress has the same units as pressure, the newton per metre squared, or the pascal (Pa).

The stress needed to break a material is called the *breaking stress* or *ultimate tensile stress*. To compare the strengths of different materials, you compare the breaking stresses, since these do not depend on the cross-sectional area of the sample you are testing. A strong material, such as steel (Figure S9), has a high ultimate tensile stress. A weak material has a low ultimate tensile stress.

A steel wire, cross-sectional area 1.0 mm², breaks under a tension of 250 N. So:

$$\text{breaking stress} = \frac{F}{A} = \frac{250 \text{ N}}{1.0 \times 10^{-6} \text{ m}^2} = 250 \text{ MPa}$$

The shape of a tension–extension graph depends on the dimensions of the sample of wire you are testing. If you have wires of the same length and the same material, the thicker wire will need a larger tension for the same extension. If the wires are of the same material and thickness, but different lengths, the longer wire will have a larger extension for the same tension.

If you wish to compare the behaviour of different materials, you need to plot quantities that do not depend on the size of the sample of material tested.

Strain, ε, (the small Greek letter 'epsilon'), is the extension divided by the original length:

$$\text{strain} = \frac{\text{extension}}{\text{original length}}$$

Strain accounts for the fact that samples stretch in proportion to their lengths. Strain has no units, since it is metres divided by metres.

For example: a steel wire 2.0 m long, stretched to just below its breaking point, extends by 2.6 mm. Then:

$$\text{strain} = \frac{\text{extension}}{\text{original length}} = \frac{2.6 \times 10^{-3} \text{ m}}{2.0 \text{ m}} = 1.3 \times 10^{-3}$$

When comparing the behaviour of materials, stress, strain and stress–strain graphs are used, since these do not depend on the size of the sample tested, only on the properties of the material tested.

Figure S9 These steel cables are able to withstand very large tensions.

Producing a stress–strain graph for a wire

When you stretch a wire elastically, the extensions are small, so you need special techniques to measure them. Use a test wire as long as possible and fix a vernier scale to it to measure the extension accurately. Hang the main scale on an identical reference wire (Figure S10). Measure the length and diameter of the test wire. Use a fixed weight to keep the reference wire taut.

Measure the extension of the test wire for a range of tensions. For each reading, calculate the stress and the strain.

Plot a graph of stress against strain and measure its slope.

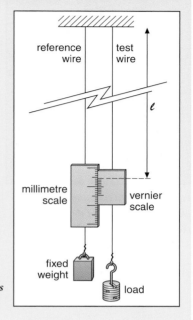

Figure S10 Measuring stress and strain for a wire.

Stress–strain graphs

Stress–strain graphs are the standard way to compare different materials under tension.

Figure S11 shows stress–strain graphs for copper and steel. Both graphs are straight lines at the beginning, showing that the strain is proportional to the stress, but each graph has a different slope.

This dotted line is a line of constant stress. For the two materials, the strain for this stress is different. The strain for copper is greatest, showing that it stretches more for a given stress; the strain for steel is less. From this you can deduce that steel is stiffer than copper, since its strain is less for a given stress.

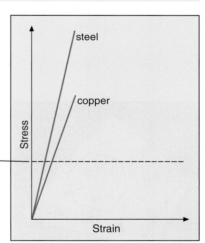

Figure S11 This stress–strain graph shows that steel is stiffer than copper.

The Young modulus

The slope of the straight-line part of the stress–strain graph for a particular material is called the Young modulus of the material:

$$\text{Young modulus} = \frac{\text{stress}}{\text{strain}}$$

$$\text{or} \quad E = \frac{\sigma}{\varepsilon}$$

Young modulus is a measure of the stiffness of the material. A stiff material has a high Young modulus.

SOLID MATERIALS

Figure S12 Field-emission electronmicrograph of the surface of platinum.

Stiffness is important for engineering materials, since for most applications it is important that the shape of a component changes very little when it is under stress. So engineering materials are often those with a high Young modulus. Obvious examples are metals, particularly steel (Table S1). For many consumer goods, stiffness is much less important. So you find flexible materials, such as polystyrene, being used for a wide range of items in which significant changes in shape in use do not matter.

Table S1 *Tensile strengths and strains at breaking*

Material	Ultimate tensile strength/MPa	Strain at breaking point	Young modulus/ GPa
Steel	250	~ 0.05	200
Copper	150	~ 0.3	120
Polystyrene	40	~ 0.03	35
Nylon	70	~ 1	2
Polyethene	20	~ 2	0.4

The structure of solids

Figure S12 shows a field-emission electronmicrograph of the surface of a metal. This gives strong evidence that metals are made of a large number of identical particles fitted together in a regular way. You know that solids and liquids are hard to compress. From this, you can deduce that the particles in solids and liquids are themselves hard to compress, and there is little space between them.

Crystals

If you have a number of identical particles and put them together, they tend to form patterns. The atoms in an element are identical. When a liquid solidifies, the particles usually arrange themselves in similar regular patterns. This means that the arrangement of atoms in most solids is not irregular – it is ordered.

A crystal is a collection of atoms with a regular structure.

The layers of atoms in a solid metal element often have a hexagonal structure like the balls in Figure S13.

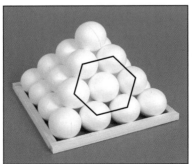

Figure S13 Stacking balls in a frame – this hexagonal structure resembles the layers of atoms in a solid metal element.

Large and small crystals

If a liquid solidifies very slowly the crystals that form are large, because there is time for the particles to arrange themselves in an ordered way. Some solids, for instance ionic solids like common salt, can solidify only in a crystalline way.

Figure S14 Crystals of tungsten metal.

If a liquid solidifies quickly crystals form in many different places, all at the same time. When all has solidified, the solid is *polycrystalline* (made of many crystals aligned in different directions). Although it is possible to make large single metal crystals, the structure of most metals is polycrystalline (Figure S15).

If a liquid solidifies very quickly there is no time for the atoms to arrange themselves regularly. This forms an amorphous solid (literally, a solid without shape). Glass is amorphous – you have to cool it very slowly in order to make crystals.

Figure S15 A polycrystalline structure is made of many crystals aligned in different directions.

Investigating structure

Break a piece of cast iron. Examine the crystals with a hand lens.

Take a crystal of calcite. Try chopping it in different directions with a hammer and razor blade. What do you deduce about the structure?

Pierce a piece of balloon rubber with a pin and try to 'stir' the pin around. Then stretch the rubber and repeat.

Stretch the rubber at right angles to the original direction and stir again.

EYE PROTECTION MUST BE WORN

Polycrystalline and amorphous solids

Most metals are polycrystalline. They are made of many crystals aligned randomly. The size of the crystals in metals depends on the rate at which metals are cooled. Slow cooling produces large crystals. Fast cooling produces small crystals. The surfaces where the crystal grains join are called *grain boundaries*.

Figure S16 shows a liquid metal sprayed onto a cold spinning cylinder to produce a thin ribbon. Under these circumstances, the cooling rate can exceed 1 MK s^{-1}. If the liquid cools so rapidly that, when it hits the cold surface, the molecules have no time to move into a crystalline structure, the resulting metal is amorphous – there is no regular arrangement of the molecules. Ultra-fast cooling can produce amorphous metals.

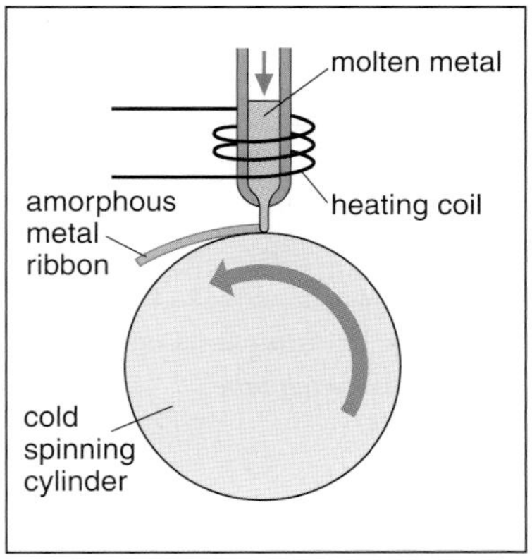

Figure S16 The jet of molten metal solidifies quickly on the cold, spinning cylinder.

Imperfections in metal crystals

If you get an absolutely perfect crystal, the uniformity would lead you to expect tremendous strength. However, getting crystals of metals perfect enough to demonstrate this theoretical strength is very difficult. Most metal crystals contain irregularities that reduce their strength considerably. The easiest type of imperfection to understand is called an edge dislocation.

SOLID MATERIALS

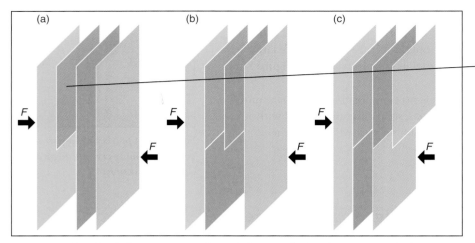

Figure S17 The edge dislocation moves through the crystal when forces are applied.

In a perfect crystal, many identical layers of atoms are stacked on top of each other. Figure S17 shows a metal crystal containing an edge dislocation. There is an additional half layer of atoms between two complete layers of atoms.

If you apply forces *F* as shown, the dislocation moves through the crystal, until it eventually stops at a grain boundary.

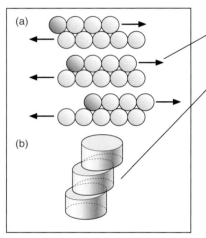

Figure S18 Certain planes of atoms can slip over each other.

Slip planes

In this simple crystal structure (Figure S18), the dislocations move along certain planes of atoms, called *slip planes*.

When the atoms are moved repeatedly, certain layers of the crystal slide over each other, without the crystal breaking apart.

Dislocations get in the way of each other

As you work a metal and it deforms plastically, the deformation produces more dislocations. As further plastic deformation takes place, the increasing numbers of dislocations moving along intersecting slip planes start to get in the way of each other. So, instead of more dislocations leading to the possibility of more plastic deformation, their tangle makes it harder for plastic deformation to take place. The material has become work-hardened.

Imperfections stop dislocation movement

The presence of atoms of a different size disrupts the crystal structure and makes it harder for dislocations to move. Carbon in steel makes it harder for the dislocations to move and hence makes the steel less able to deform plastically.

Aluminium alloys used in aircraft rely on the presence of copper and other atoms of different sizes to make the mixture of metals stronger than pure aluminium.

Grain boundaries stop dislocation movement

In a single metal crystal there are no grain boundaries. Any dislocations present can move a long way through the crystal. They allow the material to deform plastically without breaking, since only one line of bonds is being moved at a time.

In a polycrystalline material with plenty of grain boundaries, the dislocations cannot move very far. So metals with small crystals, and therefore more grain boundaries, are stronger than metals with larger crystals and fewer grain boundaries.

Stretching copper

Figure S19 shows a stress–strain graph for soft copper. The first part of the graph is a straight line. Stress is proportional to strain, and Hooke's law describes this region.

The slope of the graph is the Young modulus. For these stresses and strains, no permanent change in the structure of the copper wire occurs. As the wire is stretched, the separations of the atoms increase, but the atoms do not change position. When the stress is removed, the wire returns to its original length.

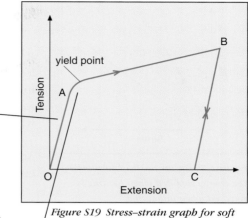

Figure S19 Stress–strain graph for soft copper.

Yielding

At point A, the copper starts to deform permanently. Above this stress, the dislocations move so that, when the stress is removed, the wire cannot return to its original shape. The stress at which permanent deformation occurs is called the *yield stress*. This is the stress at which dislocations begin to move.

Work-hardening and annealing

At point B, the wire has been stretched nearly to breaking. If the stress is then removed, the wire contracts a little, following the line BC parallel to the first part of the graph. Yet, the dislocations in the wire have become entangled and only the elastic strain is recovered. The wire is *work-hardened*.

If you test a piece of work-hardened copper, you will get a graph which is exactly like the last part of Figure S19. The value of the Young modulus remains the same.

Pulling a large-diameter copper rod through progressively smaller holes, called dies, produces copper wire. During this process, it becomes work-hardened. If it becomes too hard, it must be softened before it can be drawn into progressively thinner wire. It is heated and allowed to cool in a process called *annealing*. This gives the copper atoms sufficient energy to rearrange themselves and disentangle the dislocations. Annealing returns work-hardened copper to a soft state.

Elastic and plastic deformations

Stress is force/area, and strain is extension/(original length). So:

$$\text{stress} \times \text{strain} = \frac{\text{force}}{\text{area}} \times \frac{\text{extension}}{\text{original length}}$$

$$= \frac{\text{force} \times \text{extension}}{\text{area} \times \text{original length}}$$

$$= \frac{\text{work done}}{\text{volume}}$$

SOLID MATERIALS

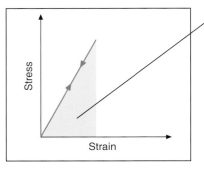

Figure S20 For an elastic deformation, the energy supplied when loading is released when unloading.

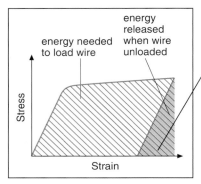

Figure S21 The energy per unit volume absorbed by the wire is the difference between the area cross-hatched in blue and the red area.

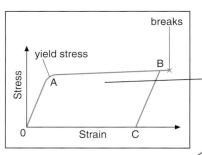

Figure S22 Stress–strain graph for soft copper.

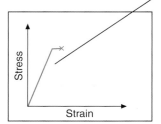

Figure S23 For work-hardened copper, the stress–strain graph is the same as the last part of the graph for soft copper.

The area under a stress–strain graph (Figure S20) is the work done per unit volume of the wire. This is called the *energy density*.

If, when you stretch and release a wire, the unloading graph is the same as the loading graph (that is, it follows the same line on the graph when loading and unloading), then energy density for stretching is the same as for unstretching. So, all the energy put in to stretching the wire is returned when the wire is released. The atoms go back to their original positions.

An *elastic deformation* is one in which no energy is absorbed during a complete stretching/unstretching cycle. When elastically deformed,

$$\text{energy density} = \tfrac{1}{2} \times \text{stress} \times \text{strain}$$

If the unloading graph is not the same as the loading graph (Figure S21), less energy is released when the wire is unloaded than was needed to load the wire. Some energy is absorbed and permanent deformation is produced. Dislocations have moved the atoms to different positions. This is called *plastic deformation*.

This plastic behaviour shows that copper's dislocations can move easily. Copper is *ductile*: it can be pulled out into wires. It is also malleable: it can be beaten into the required shape.

Tough or brittle

Metals are chosen for a combination of their elastic and plastic qualities. For instance, we do not want a car to distort so much when it is full of passengers that its doors will not shut! Using a stiff material, such as steel, when constructing a car's body controls the amount of elastic deformation. But cars are also designed to absorb large amounts of energy by plastic deformation during a car crash, by allowing certain regions to crumple.

Soft copper (Figure S22) is tough: the area under the graph before it breaks is large. It absorbs large amounts of energy per unit volume before it breaks.

Work-hardened copper (Figure S23) is brittle. The area under the stress–strain graph is small. It absorbs little energy by plastic deformation before breaking. This is because the dislocations have become entangled and cannot cause further plastic deformation.

The behaviour of steels

Steels are usually produced by mixing iron with varying proportions of carbon. Steels are widely used as engineering materials. They are stiff and relatively cheap. By changing the amount of carbon and the heat treatment they receive, they can be given a wide range of properties.

Mild steel contains less than 0.25% carbon. The steel used for car bodies contains 0.04 to 0.08% carbon. Its behaviour depends little on its heat treatment. Figure S24 shows a stress–strain graph for mild steel. As with the behaviour of copper, the graph shows elastic behaviour for low stresses, followed by plastic behaviour for larger stresses.

The behaviour of high-carbon steel depends on heat treatment. If it is heated and cooled rapidly by quenching it in cold water (quench-hardened), it changes its crystal structure to one in which dislocations cannot move very far, and the steel is hard but brittle. It is used for cutting tools like chisels. Figure S25 shows a graph for quench-hardened high-carbon steel.

If the quench-hardened steel is then reheated slightly and allowed to cool, the crystal structure begins to change and the steel becomes less hard. It can then be used for hammers and screwdrivers. This softening process is called tempering.

There is a wide range of steels from mild steel to high-carbon steel and they have a range of different properties. Engineers choose the carbon content for the job in hand. Whereas low-carbon steels are used for car bodies, for which the ability to bend and absorb energy is important, medium-carbon steels, with heat treatment, give greater strength for structural components and high-carbon steels produce very strong but brittle tools and twist drills.

Comparing copper and steel

Figure S26 compares the stress–strain graphs for soft copper and mild steel. The strength of a material is the stress required to break a material. Steel is stronger than copper.

A stiff or rigid material has a high Young modulus: it takes a high stress to produce a given strain. A flexible material has a low Young modulus: it needs a low stress for a given strain. Figure S26 shows that steel is stiffer than copper: the slope of the stress–strain graph is greater. The Young modulus is a function of atomic bonding: strong bonds produce stiff materials.

Creep and fatigue

Materials can fail due to plastic deformation occurring below the yield stress.

Creep occurs if the strain of a material increases over time, even though the stress remains constant. A loaded material creeps if it is above about 0.3 of its Kelvin melting temperature. For instance, lead sheeting (melting point ~ 600 K) on sloping roofs creeps; it gradually stretches over time.

If you continually load and unload a material, it can fail, even if the stresses are less than the yield stress. The loading and unloading can produce cracks that gradually get bigger with time. The material eventually breaks. This is called *fatigue*. Fatigue is a big problem with all aluminium alloys used for aircraft bodies. After a time, microscopic cracks build up and, although it may look safe, the airframe can no longer cope with the stresses for which it was designed.

With experience of the material, engineers are able to predict fatigue failure, and components are changed before failure occurs.

Both creep and fatigue occur because dislocation movement is a statistical process. At low temperatures and stresses, dislocation movement is less likely but it may still slowly occur.

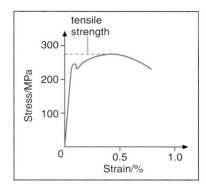

Figure S24 Stress–strain graph for mild steel.

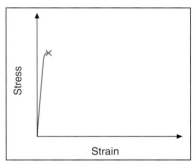

Figure S25 Stress–strain for quench-hardened steel.

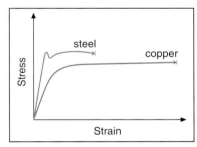

Figure S26 Steel is stiffer than copper: the slope of the stress–strain graph is greater.

Polymers

Carbon can join with other atoms to form long-chain molecules called *polymers*. Some polymers, like rubber, starch and cellulose, occur naturally; other polymers are man-made.

If the molecules of a polymer are randomly arranged, the polymer is amorphous. If the arrangement is partly random and partly ordered, the polymer is semicrystalline. It is not possible to make perfectly crystalline polymers.

Thermoplastics

The molecules in a polymer are strong. The bonds *along* the chains are hard to break. But these bonds are not the only bonds within polymers. There are forces *between* the chains in a polymer.

In some polymers, the only bonds between the chains are weak forces called *van der Waals forces*. At low temperatures, the van der Waals forces restrict movement of the chains, but at higher temperatures, the molecules have sufficient energy to rotate or move past each other. This allows the chains to rearrange.

These polymers are called *thermoplastics*. They are elastic at low temperatures, but become plastic at higher temperatures when the van der Waals bonds break. Thermoplastics are widely used for moulding consumer items (Figure S27). They are usually delivered to a manufacturer as sacks of granules, which can be heated to melt them before they are injected into a mould, or extruded (squeezed through a nozzle) to produce a finished item.

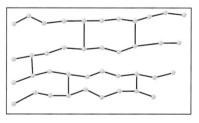

Figure S27 This electric kettle is made from extruded thermoplastic.

Thermosets

In some plastics, there are strong, permanent links between the chains, called *crosslinks* (Figure S28). Such links fix the arrangement of the polymer chains at all temperatures. These plastics are called *thermosets*. Thermosets are rigid, whatever the temperature. In the first thermosets, the crosslinks were formed by a chemical reaction that was triggered by temperature: hence, the name 'thermosets'. Today, there are many thermosets that have crosslinks formed at low temperatures.

Figure S28 Crosslinks create a fixed arrangement in a linear polymer.

Amorphous thermoplastics

Perspex is a typical amorphous thermoplastic. Its chains have no order in their arrangement. Figure S29 shows a transparent telephone made of Perspex. It is rigid at room temperature, because the chains are not free to move.

Figure S29 The components of this telephone can be seen through its Perspex case.

The *red* line on Figure S30 shows a stress–strain graph for Perspex at room temperature. Perspex obeys Hooke's law and is elastic. If you remove the stress, the Perspex will return to its original shape. If Perspex at room temperature is stretched beyond its elastic limit, it will break. At room temperature, Perspex is brittle – its behaviour is like glass.

If you increase the temperature of Perspex, you weaken the van der Waals bonding. Eventually, you reach the *glass transition temperature*. Below this temperature, Perspex behaves like glass. It will bounce like a glass marble, but will shatter if hit too hard.

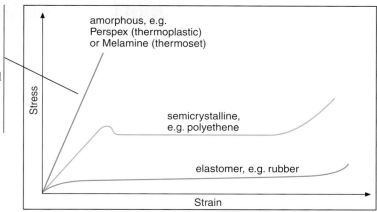

Figure S30 Stress–strain graph for a range of polymers.

Around the glass transition temperature, you can distort Perspex, but then it gradually returns to its original shape. The movement of the chains is very viscous and they absorb energy when they move. A Perspex ball at the glass transition temperature has a very poor bounce.

Above the glass transition temperature, Perspex is rubbery. It will bounce like a rubber ball. If you increase the temperature further, Perspex gets softer, eventually loses its shape and can be moulded.

Semicrystalline thermoplastics

Polyethene (polythene or polyethylene) and nylon are typical semicrystalline thermoplastics. In both, there is some regular arrangement of the chain molecules. The arrangement of the chains depends on the way that the polymer is made and shaped.

The *green* line on Figure S30 shows a stress–strain graph for polyethene. During the first part of the graph, polyethene is elastic and obeys Hooke's law. As the stress increases, polyethene distorts plastically. In the tangled, amorphous regions, the chains stretch out along the direction of the tension (Figure S31). As the stretching proceeds, the chains become more aligned. At this stage, it is harder to stretch polyethene and the graph becomes steeper.

If the stress is removed after stretching, the polyethene does not return to its original length, but remains with the chains still partly uncoiled.

Cold-drawn polyethene tape is used for strapping boxes. It consists of polyethene in which all the chains lie along the length of the tape. It is very hard to stretch cold-drawn polyethene tape, because the molecules are strong. But it is easy to pull it apart sideways, because the bonds between the chains are very weak.

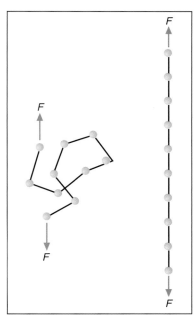

Figure S31 It is easier to stretch a coiled molecule than a straight one.

Rigid thermosets

Epoxy resin and Melamine are two typical thermosetting plastics. Epoxy resin is commonly used as an adhesive. It is made from a viscous liquid of chain molecules. Strong and permanent crosslinks form when a chemical hardener is added producing a very strong and rigid plastic. Melamine is another thermoset sometimes used to make the durable surface of kitchen worktops.

Thermosetting plastics cannot be distorted at higher temperatures. Their strong permanent crosslinks are much stronger than the weak van der Waals bonds in thermoplastics. Once they have been formed, their shape is fixed and cannot be changed without destroying the structure, e.g. by machining. Thermosets are amorphous. They cannot undergo plastic deformation, so they are brittle. They have graphs similar to the *red* line in Figure S30.

The behaviour of rubber

Elastomers

An elastomer is a material that returns to its original shape when a distorting force is removed. Rubber is an elastomer. It is an amorphous polymer with some crosslinks. In unstretched rubber, the long chains are coiled and tangled up. As you stretch the rubber, the chains straighten.

For rubber, extension is not proportional to tension. So a stress–strain graph is very far from a straight line. The shape of the graph in Figure S32 gives you some idea of what is happening inside the rubber as you stretch it.

When you apply small tensions to the rubber, you start straightening out the tangle of chain molecules. This is a relatively easy process; the rubber is not stiff, and it needs a comparatively small stress for a given strain.

As the extension of the rubber band increases, the chains become straighter and are then harder to stretch. The rubber is then stiffer; it needs a larger stress for a given strain.

When you remove the load from a rubber band, it returns more or less to its original length. But the unloading graph is below the loading graph.

The area under the stress–strain graph is the work done per unit volume, the energy density. The work done per unit volume on the rubber when it is stretched (the *blue* hatched area) is greater than the work done per unit volume by the rubber when it returns to its original length (the *red* area).

The area between the two graphs is the energy absorbed per unit volume during the stretching and releasing process.

This behaviour is called *hysteresis*. Each time the rubber is stretched and released, energy is absorbed by the rubber. It makes the rubber hot, which then heats the surroundings. Hysteresis losses in rubber tyres account for a proportion of the energy needed to power a car.

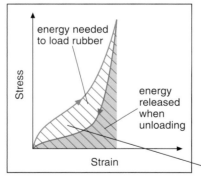

Figure S32 Stress–strain graph for rubber: the work done on the rubber to stretch it is greater than the work done by the rubber as it returns to its original shape.

Materials technology

Combining materials

Many pure materials are strong, but their individual properties are not fit for every task. Materials technologists (the people who make the materials), combine different materials to make the best use of their different properties.

Stopping cracks

You know that cracks reduce the strength of many objects. A crack in a glass window can spread right across it. Ships have sunk as a result of cracks spreading right across them.

If part of an object in tension is cracked, the stress will concentrate at the point of the crack. The material will fail at this stress concentration and the crack will get bigger. You can relieve stress concentrations by drilling a hole at the end of a crack. This helps to prevent the crack from spreading (Figure S33).

You can reduce the danger of cracks by using a material that can undergo plastic deformation and survive the cracks. Tough materials in which dislocations are free to move, like copper and mild steel, are less troubled by cracks than brittle materials like glass or cast iron.

Reinforced concrete

Concrete is cheap and moderately strong in compression. Steel is quite cheap and strong in tension and compression. If you put steel rods in concrete, then the steel can take the tension and the concrete can take the compression. Reinforced concrete beams are used to span gaps in walls. When a load is placed on the beam, it bends (Figure S34). The bottom of the beam is under tension and the top is under compression. Reinforced beams in this situation have the steel at the bottom to take the tension, and the concrete at the top takes the compression.

Pre-stressed, reinforced concrete is an improvement on normal reinforced concrete. With normal reinforced concrete, the reinforcing rods hold the structure together when tension is applied to that part, but, as the steel stretches, the concrete around it cracks.

With pre-stressed concrete, the steel reinforcements are first stretched (Figure S35). Concrete is then cast around the stretched reinforcements. When the concrete is set, the stretching force is removed from the reinforcements and these contract, putting the concrete into compression.

When pre-stressed beams are used, loads applied cause the reinforcements to be stretched again, but not enough to remove all the compressive stress on the concrete. The result is that the concrete never gets into tension and therefore never cracks.

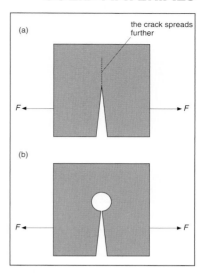

Figure S33 (a) Stress concentration causes crack to spread; (b) Stress concentration relieved by drilling a hole at the end of the crack.

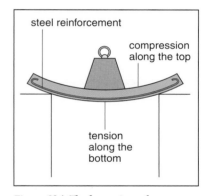

Figure S34 The beam is under compression at the top and under tension at the bottom.

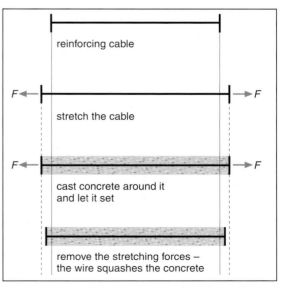

Figure S35 Making pre-stressed, reinforced concrete.

SOLID MATERIALS

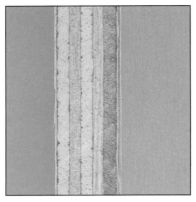 

Figure S36 (a) Plywood has grain going in opposite directions; (b) chipboard has grain going randomly in all directions.

Other composite materials

Wood is strong in tension along the grain and weak across the grain. It is comparatively weak in compression because the fibres collapse. Plywood is made from alternate layers of wood with the grain going in opposite directions (Figure S36(a)) – this gives it good strength in both directions. Chipboard has chips of wood randomly oriented and glued together to give strength in all directions (Figure S36(b)).

Rigid thermosetting polymers are strong, but brittle. They can be reinforced by mixing strong fibres in them before they harden. In glass-reinforced plastic (GRP), glass fibres are mixed into a synthetic resin such as epoxy. This produces a composite material that is strong and tough. Carbon-fibre-reinforced composites are even stronger (Figure S37). Toughness depends on the interface between the fibres and the resin being comparatively weak, so that the crack is blunted when it meets the interface. The interfaces act as crack stoppers.

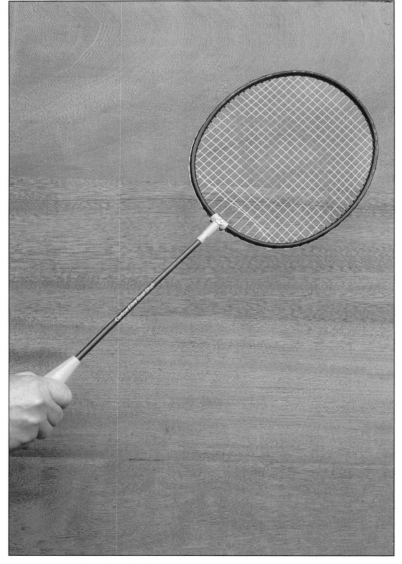

Figure S37 Carbon-fibre badminton racquet – a mixture of materials to produce maximum strength.

Nuclear and Particle Physics

Inside the nucleus

In this Option, you will learn about the particles that make up the matter from which the physical world is made. You already know a little about these particles. The atom, for example, is made of protons, neutrons and electrons. And most of the mass is in the tiny nucleus, located in the centre of the atom.

Firing beams of electrons at matter (Figure NP1) allows us to determine what particles make up the nucleus of that matter.

Figure NP1 The Stanford linear accelerator is 3 km long and can accelerate electrons to 50 GeV.

Density of nuclear matter

The nucleus is made of protons and neutrons which are very close to each other. The number of protons and neutrons in the nucleus is the nucleon number, A. More massive nuclei have more nucleons in the nucleus. They have more mass and more volume. Their nuclear densities are about the same.

The simplest nucleus is the hydrogen nucleus (Figure NP2). It has one proton. Its mass is the mass of the proton, and its volume is $\frac{4}{3}\pi r_0{}^3$, where r_0 is the radius of the proton.

A larger nucleus with A nucleons has a radius r (Figure NP3). Its volume is $\frac{4}{3}\pi r^3$. You can estimate that the volume is A times as big as the volume of the hydrogen nucleus, the volume is $A\frac{4}{3}\pi r_0{}^3$.

$$\text{So } \frac{4}{3}\pi r^3 = A\frac{4}{3}\pi r_0{}^3$$
$$r^3 = A\,r_0{}^3$$
$$\therefore r = r_0\sqrt[3]{A} = r_0 A^{\frac{1}{3}}$$

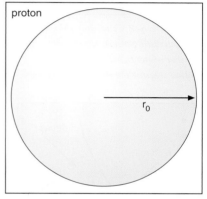

Figure NP2 The hydrogen nucleus: the volume of the hydrogen nucleus is $\frac{4}{3}\pi r_0{}^3$.

The radii of nuclei are proportional to the cube root of the nucleon number.

Forces between protons

Protons and neutrons are very close together in the nucleus. Protons are positively charged. Since they are close together, they must repel each other very strongly.

This electrostatic force between the protons does not succeed in making the protons in the nucleus fly apart – so there must be another force that holds them together. This force is called the *strong nuclear force*.

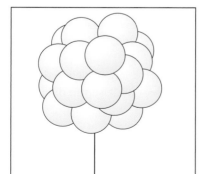

Figure NP3 A larger nucleus: the volume of this larger nucleus is $\frac{4}{3}\pi r^3$.

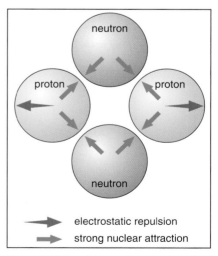

Figure NP4 Repulsion and attraction: the strong nuclear force holds the nucleus together, against the electrostatic repulsion.

The strong nuclear forces bind the protons and neutrons together. The neutrons hold the protons just far enough apart so that the attractive strong force between the protons is equal to the repulsive electrostatic force (Figure NP4).

The **electrostatic repulsion** acts between protons even when they are a long distance apart. It is a **long-range** force. The **strong nuclear force** acts *only* between protons and neutrons that are **close together**. It is a short-range force.

Stable and unstable nuclei

In stable nuclei, the strong forces within the nucleus are sufficient to keep them together all the time. But you know from *Mechanics and Radioactivity* that many nuclei are unstable. Occasionally, parts of the nucleus fly apart, emitting nuclear particles.

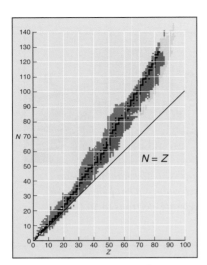

Figure NP5 N–Z trend line: shows a characteristic pattern when the number of neutrons in a nucleus is plotted against the number of protons.

Figure NP5 shows a graph of the numbers of neutrons, N, against the proton numbers, Z, for all nuclei. The black dots on the graph are the stable nuclei; the blue, red and yellow dots are the unstable nuclei. The graph shows a distinct pattern. For the nuclides with low proton numbers, the number of neutrons is similar to the number of protons. The nuclides are clustered around the line $N = Z$. As the proton number increases, the number of neutrons exceeds the number of protons.

The black dots in Figure NP5 show a trend line for stable nuclei. This trend line is drawn in Figure NP6. There are no plots in Figure NP5 a long way from the trend line. This implies that such nuclides are never formed or are not stable. In general, nuclide plots that are some way from the trend line come closer to the trend line when they decay; that is, they tend to become more stable. Nuclides that are at the top of the trend line are unstable and decay down the trend line.

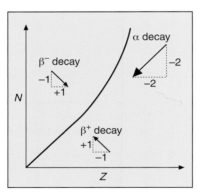

Figure NP6 Radioactive decay brings the nuclide plot closer to the trend line.

When alpha decay occurs, both N and Z decrease by 2. This causes the atom to move diagonally down in the general direction of the origin, as shown in Figure NP6. Alpha emitters are yellow plots in Figure NP5.

With β^- decay, N decreases by 1 and Z increases by 1. The atom moves diagonally down, towards the trend line, the blue plots in Figure NP5. With β^+ decay, N increases by 1 and Z decreases by 1. The atom moves diagonally up, towards the trend line. These are the red plots in Figure NP5.

Figure NP7 shows a typical sequence of decays by which a large nuclide decays along the trend line from a massive nuclide to a smaller one. Use the data to plot an N–Z curve for this decay sequence.

Binding energy

If you assemble a small nuclide out of separate protons and electrons, energy is released. This energy is called the **binding energy**. If you want to separate a nucleus again into the separate particles, you have to supply this energy to the nucleus.

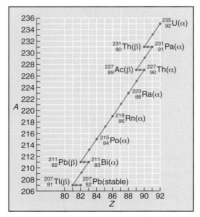

Figure NP7 Decay chain.

Like all energy, the binding energy has mass m, given by the formula:

$$m = \frac{E}{c^2}$$

where E is the energy and c is the speed of light. This means that you can find the mass equivalent to the binding energy by subtracting the mass of a nucleus from the total mass of the separate particles. The difference is called the **mass defect**.

For example, the mass of a proton is 1.007 276 u and the mass of a neutron is 1.008 665 u. Two protons and two neutrons together make a helium nucleus (an alpha particle), which has a mass of 4.002 603 u. So we can work out the mass defect and find the binding energy, as follows:

mass of protons	$= 2 \times 1.007\,276\,\text{u}$	$= 2.014\,552\,\text{u}$
mass of neutrons	$= 2 \times 1.008\,665\,\text{u}$	$= 2.017\,330\,\text{u}$
total mass of protons plus neutons		$= 4.031\,882\,\text{u}$
mass of nucleus		$= 4.002\,603\,\text{u}$
mass defect		$= 0.029\,279\,\text{u}$
		$= 0.029\,279 \times 1.66 \times 10^{-27}\,\text{kg}$
		$= 4.86 \times 10^{-29}\,\text{kg}$

$$
\begin{aligned}
\text{binding energy of helium nucleus } E &= mc^2 \\
&= 4.86 \times 10^{-29}\,\text{kg} \times (3 \times 10^8\,\text{m s}^{-1})^2 \\
&= 4.4 \times 10^{-12}\,\text{J}
\end{aligned}
$$

Binding energy per nucleon

If you divide the binding energy of a nuclide by the number of nucleons in that nuclide, you get the binding energy per nucleon. Figure NP8 shows the binding energy per nucleon plotted against mass number for nuclides of different mass numbers. This shows how much energy is given out per nucleon for a given mass number. The most stable nuclides are those with the most binding energy per nucleon; but you can see that the binding energy per nucleon changes relatively little from mass number 60 to mass number 100.

Radioactive dating

Think about a pure sample of ^{235}U. As the decay series shows in Figure NP7, the uranium gradually decays into other elements. So the proportion of these other elements increases with time, and the proportion of uranium decreases. If you measure the proportion of other elements present, you can work out how long ago the sample of uranium was pure.

This process – working out an age for a sample from the proportion of the isotopes present – is called *radioactive dating*. Radioactive dating is an important historical tool. You may have heard of carbon-14 dating of old objects. The most common isotope of carbon is carbon-12. Carbon-14 is an unstable isotope naturally produced in the Earth's atmosphere.

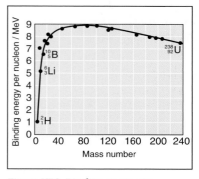

Figure NP8 Binding energy per nucleon.

Figure NP9 Carbon-14 dating showed that the shroud of Turin dates from the Middle Ages.

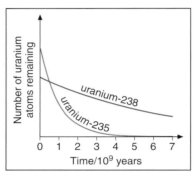

Figure NP10 ^{235}U has a shorter half-life than ^{238}U.

Living organisms take in carbon and, while they are alive, the proportion of carbon-14 to carbon-12 in them is the same as in the Earth's atmosphere. When these organisms die, they are no longer taking in new carbon-14 from the atmosphere, so the amount of carbon-14 decreases with time. If we assume that the proportion of carbon-14 in the atmosphere has remained constant, we can estimate the age of a material by measuring the proportion of carbon-14 to carbon-12. The shroud of Turin (Figure NP9) was recently dated using carbon-14 dating.

Other types of radioactive dating can be used to estimate the age of older objects. Present astrophysical theories indicate that both ^{235}U and ^{238}U are produced in the ratio 0.7 : 1 when some stars (supernovae) explode. The ratio of these isotopes on Earth is 138 : 1. Figure NP10 shows why this ratio has increased with time.

The half-life of ^{235}U is much less than the half-life of ^{238}U. Over the period since the formation of the Earth, much more ^{235}U would have decayed than ^{238}U. If you assume that the ratio at the beginning was 0.7, you can use the half-lives of the two isotopes to calculate how long it takes for this ratio to increase to 138. Using this method, an estimate of about 6500 million years is obtained for the age of the Earth!

Of course, this estimate assumes that the Earth was formed from material left behind by an exploding star and that the half-lives of the two isotopes of uranium have always been the same. This may or may not have been the case, and we cannot be sure of such matters because no one was there to observe it!

Decay of n and p within the nucleus

Nuclear decay

About one hundred years ago, physicists and chemists arrived at a simple understanding of the world. They had discovered protons and electrons, and guessed at the existence of the neutron. But before the neutron was found, this simple model of the nucleus was complicated by evidence for another particle, the neutrino. (You will see later that the particle involved is actually an antineutrino.)

You learned in *Mechanics and Radioactivity* that, in β^- decay, a neutron in the nucleus splits into a proton and an electron.

Neutron $\Rightarrow$ proton + electron + energy

The mass of the neutron is greater than the mass of the proton plus the mass of the electron. The difference in mass is the mass of the energy released. This is simplest to follow if the unit of mass used is the unified mass unit, u. The unified mass unit is chosen so that the masses of both the proton and the neutron are about 1 u. The mass of an electron is about $\frac{1}{2000}$ u, more closely 0.000554 u. The unified mass unit has a value of 1.66×10^{-27} kg.

Mass of neutron = mass of proton + mass of electron + mass of energy

1.00867 u   = 1.00728 u   + 0.00055 u   + 0.00084 u

The mass of the energy emitted is 0.00084 u.

Energy has mass, so it can be 'weighed' just like any other quantity which has mass. But energy is also measured in other units. Large amounts of energy can be measured in joules. Small amounts of energy can be measured in electronvolts:

$$1 \text{ eV} = 1.6 \times 10^{-19} \text{ J}$$

The mass of this energy is 1.07×10^{-9} u. Larger energies are measured in millions of electronvolts (MeV) or in giga electron volts ($1 \text{ GeV} = 10^9 \text{ eV}$). Particle physicists often use electronvolts as a unit of mass. The mass of 930 MeV (just under 1 GeV) is 1 u.

If the equation above is expressed in energy units:

Mass of neutron = mass of proton + mass of electron + mass of energy

938.06 MeV   = 936.77 MeV   + 0.51 MeV   + 0.78 MeV

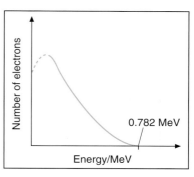

Figure NP11 The energy spectrum of β⁻ particles.

The missing energy

When β⁻ decay takes place, the proton is trapped in the nucleus. The emitted electron should have kinetic energy of 0.782 MeV. But most β electrons have much less energy, as Figure NP11 shows. This graph is called the *energy spectrum* for β⁻ decay.

To account for the missing energy, it was suggested that a neutral particle of very low mass is emitted at the same time and carries away the rest of the energy. The emitted particle must have low mass, since some electrons account for nearly all the energy. The particle must be neutral, because it leaves no track in a detector. This particle was given the name *antineutrino*. Its symbol, $\bar{\nu}$, is shown in Table NP1, along with symbols for other common particles. So the full equation for β⁻ decay is:

n   p + e⁻ + ν̄

Table NP1 *Some common particles and antiparticles, with their symbols*

Type of particle	Particle and its Antiparticle	Symbol
Leptons	electron	e⁻
	positron	e⁺
	neutrino	ν
	antineutrino	ν̄
	muon	μ⁻
	antimuon	μ⁺
Hadrons	neutron	n
	antineutron	n̄
	proton	p
	antiproton	p̄
Quarks	up quark	u
	anti-up quark	ū
	down quark	d
	anti-down quark	d̄

You know from *Mechanics and Radioactivity* that some artificially-created nuclei decay by β^+ emission. The β^+, or positron, behaves exactly like an electron with a positive charge. The energy spectrum for β^+ decay is like that for β^- decay. The emitted β^+ particle has a range of energies. This again suggests the presence of another particle – the neutrino, ν. So the full equation for β^+ is:

$$p \Rightarrow n + e^+ + \nu$$

The energy released during β^+ decay is derived from the whole nucleus that decays, not just from the individual proton.

The energy spectrum of alpha decay

When alpha decay takes place, the emitted particles have a clearly defined energy. This shows that alpha decay does not involve any particles other than the alpha particle and the nucleus.

The neutrino and antineutrino

β^- and β^+ decays are the first two indications that there are particles other than the proton, neutron and electron. They reveal the neutrino, ν, and the antineutrino, $\bar{\nu}$. There are other particles that make up matter.

Particles and antiparticles

The electron and the positron are examples of two particles that are a special type of pair. One is charged positively, the other is charged negatively. They both have the same mass. You can think of the positron as being the 'opposite of' an electron. The positron is called the *antiparticle* of the electron. Similarly, the electron is the *antiparticle* of the positron. Together, the two are called a *particle–antiparticle* pair.

The neutrino and the antineutrino are also a particle–antiparticle pair.

Annihilation of particles

When a particle meets its antiparticle, they annihilate each other. Both particles disappear and energy is released as a photon of electromagnetic radiation. As you would expect, the mass of the energy released is equal to the mass of the two particles annihilating each other.

In energy units, the mass of an electron is 0.51 MeV. So is the mass of a positron. So, when an electron and a positron meet:

electron + positron $\Rightarrow$ energy of a photon

0.51 MeV + 0.51 MeV $\Rightarrow$ 1.02 MeV

In the next section, you will meet the antiproton. This, like the proton, has a mass of 930 MeV. When proton meets an antiproton:

p $\quad$ + $\bar{p}$ $\quad\quad$ $\Rightarrow$ energy

930 MeV + 930 MeV $\Rightarrow$ 1860 MeV

Fundamental particles

Great fleas have little fleas
upon their backs to bite 'em
And little fleas have lesser fleas
and so ad infinitum.

(Augustus deMorgan 1806–1871)

A fundamental particle is one which cannot be split into anything smaller. It has no internal structure or components.

You can see from β decay, that both the proton and the neutron can decay. So you cannot regard them as fundamental particles. It might lead you to think that all particles can be split up and there might be no fundamental particles. But, so far, it seems that certain particles really are indivisible and can be called fundamental.

Leptons

Electrons, positrons, neutrinos and antineutrinos are light particles called *leptons* (light ones). They have never been split apart into smaller components. They seem to be fundamental particles and they seem to have no radius: they are like a point.

Hadrons

The nucleons (protons and neutrons) are relatively heavy, and are called *hadrons* (heavy ones). Protons and neutrons have a detectable radius. If you collide them with each other, you can detect that they have internal structure. They consist of smaller fundamental particles called *quarks*. These particles are shown in Table NP1.

Quarks

Evidence for quarks comes from firing electrons at protons (hydrogen nuclei) to probe the distribution of charge within the proton. If the charge is uniform, the electrostatic field around the proton should be uniform and the electrons should scatter elastically. Low-energy electrons do scatter in this way (Figure NP12a) and the protons recoil as predicted. But above a particular energy, the protons deflect some electrons through large angles. The recoiling electron has much less energy, and a jet of fundamental particles is emitted (Figure NP12b). This is like the nucleus scattering α particles. This scattering is deep; it probes deep into the structure of matter. It is also inelastic; the electron does not bounce off. The electron has sufficient energy to shatter the proton into a jet of hadrons.

If protons can do this to electrons, it suggests that the charge in the protons is not uniform but split between even smaller charged particles. These particles are called *quarks* (which rhymes with either 'pork' or 'park'!).

Leptons and quarks can be arranged in a simple pattern according to their electric charge (Table NP2). The electron and its neutrino are associated with two quarks, called up and down (u and d). These both carry electric charge. But the charge of the up quark is $+\frac{2}{3}$ of the electronic charge e and that of the down quark is $-\frac{1}{3}$ of e.

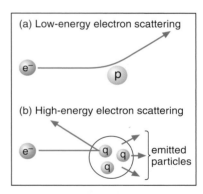

Figure NP12 Deep inelastic scattering reveals that the proton has structure.

Table NP2 *The pattern of electric charges of leptons and quarks (in units of electronic charge e)*

Leptons		Quarks	
neutral	0	positive	$+\frac{2}{3}$
negative	−1	negative	$-\frac{1}{3}$

Table NP3 *The four fundamental particles of matter in the universe today*

Leptons		Quarks	
ν_e	0	u	$+\frac{2}{3}$
e^-	−1	d	$-\frac{1}{3}$

This family of four particles makes up almost all of the matter in the universe (Table NP3). There are no particles with charges of $+\frac{2}{3}$ or $-\frac{1}{3}$ in the everyday world, because quarks can exist only within hadrons where the charges always balance out to a whole number.

Tables NP2 and NP3 do not include the positron, e^+ (a lepton with exactly the same mass as an electron but with charge $+1$). Putting it beside the electron upsets the symmetry of the pattern and suggests that there is an *up-quark* with an opposite charge of $-\frac{2}{3}$, and a *down-quark* with charge $+\frac{1}{3}$. These particles, having the same mass as e^-, u and d but with opposite charge, are called *antiparticles*. They are mostly shown with a bar over the symbol, but some antileptons are shown by their charge (see Table NP1). An antineutrino $\bar{\nu}$ completes the symmetry.

First-generation particles

The masses of quarks cannot be found directly and are estimated, for comparison, with the leptons. The four particles and their four equivalent antiparticles (Table NP4) together are called the *first generation*.

The neutrinos are associated particularly with the e^- and e^+ and are shown by subscripts: ν_e and $\bar{\nu}_e$.

Second-generation particles

In 1937, another particle was discovered in cosmic rays from outer space. This particle was just like an electron, but was 200 times more massive. Experiments found another complete generation of particles that look exactly like more massive versions of the first generation. The massive electron is called a *muon* μ^- and it has its own *muon neutrino* ν_μ. The two more massive quarks are called *charm* and *strange* (c and s). Each of these particles has its own antiparticle, and together they make up the second generation (Table NP5).

Third-generation particles

In 1975, an even more massive lepton was discovered, matched by another massive quark in 1977. This suggested a third generation of massive particles and antiparticles, called the *tau* τ^-, *tau neutrino* ν_τ, and top and bottom quarks (t and b). The very massive top quark was confirmed in 1996 (Table NP6).

Theoretical and experimental results indicate that there are no more generations, but cannot yet explain why there are three, or why the particles within them have the masses they do.

Hadrons

Quarks rarely occur alone. They usually occur in combinations of two or three, forming the *hadrons*. There are three types of hadrons (TableNP7): mesons have one quark and one antiquark ($q\bar{q}$); baryons have three quarks (qqq); antibaryons have three antiquarks ($\bar{q}\bar{q}\bar{q}$).

Table NP4 *First-generation particles*

Leptons		Quarks	
$\bar{\nu}_e$	ν_e	u	$\bar{u}$
0.0 GeV*		0.33 GeV	
e^+	e^-	d	$\bar{d}$
5.11×10^{-4} GeV		0.34 GeV	

*Neutrinos may have a very small but not negligible mass

Table NP5 *Second-generation particles*

Leptons		Quarks	
$\bar{\nu}_\mu$	ν_μ	c	$\bar{c}$
0.0 GeV*		1.58 GeV	
μ^+	μ^-	s	$\bar{s}$
0.106 GeV		0.47 GeV	

*Neutrinos have a very small but not negligible mass

Table NP6 *Third-generation particles*

Leptons		Quarks	
$\bar{\nu}_\tau$	ν_τ	t	$\bar{t}$
0.0 GeV*		180 GeV	
τ^+	τ^-	b	$\bar{b}$
1.78 GeV		4.58 GeV	

*Neutrinos may have a small but negligible mass

Table NP7 *Examples of hadrons*

Mesons	Symbol	$q\bar{q}$	Charge
pi minus	π^-	$d\bar{u}$	−1
eta zero	η^0	$s\bar{s}$	0
D plus	D^+	$c\bar{d}$	+1

Baryons	Symbol	qqq	Charge
delta double plus	Δ^{++}	uuu	+2
proton	p	uud	+1
neutron	n	udd	0
omega minus	Ω^-	sss	−1

Antibaryons	Symbol	$\bar{q}\,\bar{q}\,\bar{q}$	Charge
antiproton	$\bar{p}$	$\bar{u}\,\bar{u}\,\bar{d}$	−1
antilambda	$\bar{\Lambda}$	$\bar{u}\,\bar{d}\,\bar{s}$	0

The masses of the hadrons are known from observations. But these cannot be used to find precise masses for the quarks they contain, because energy is released when quarks bind together in the same way that binding energy is released when nucleons form nuclei (see *Waves and Our Universe*). Hadrons have less mass than the separate quarks, but the size of the binding energy is unknown. In addition, some mesons and baryons can exist in excited states that appear to be more massive than usual.

Only four mesons, called π mesons (pions), can be made from the first generation of quarks: $d\bar{u}$, $d\bar{d}$, $u\bar{u}$ and $u\bar{d}$. Adding s and $\bar{s}$ quarks allows the formation of another five mesons (Table NP8).

Table NP8 *The nine mesons (light backgrounds) made from u, d and s quarks and antiquarks (dark backgrounds), showing their charge and mass*

Quarks	Antiquarks		
	$\bar{d}$ $+\frac{1}{3}$	$\bar{u}$ $-\frac{2}{3}$	$\bar{s}$ $+\frac{1}{3}$
d $-\frac{1}{3}$	$d\bar{d}$ π^0 0.135 GeV	$d\bar{u}$ π^- 0.140 GeV	$d\bar{s}$ K^0 0.498 GeV
u $+\frac{2}{3}$	$u\bar{d}$ π^+ 0.140 GeV	$u\bar{u}$ π^0 0.135 GeV	$u\bar{s}$ K^+ 0.494 GeV
s $-\frac{1}{3}$	$s\bar{d}$ $\bar{K}^0$ 0.498 GeV	$s\bar{u}$ K^- 0.494 GeV	$s\bar{s}$ η^0 0.958 GeV

Pions commonly occur in particle collisions, because they contain the quarks with the lowest masses and so are produced more easily than more massive particles. The second- and third-generation quarks and antiquarks make mesons in the same way, with the same pattern of charges. But these more massive mesons are observed less frequently, if at all, in collisions. Mesons can also be formed by quarks from different generations, giving 36 possibilities.

For example, a $u\bar{b}$ meson has charges of $+\frac{2}{3}$ and $+\frac{1}{3}$, making an overall charge of +1. Particles containing a strange or charm quark (s, $\bar{s}$, or c, $\bar{c}$) are often called strange or charmed particles: they are similar to those with u or d quarks, but they have greater masses and are usually much less stable.

You could also draw up tables of baryons (qqq) or antibaryons ($\overline{qqq}$), giving well over 200 possibilities. The proton and neutron are important. They contain u and d quarks from the first generation. The proton has a charge of $+1$, so must have two charges of $+\dfrac{2}{3}$ and one charge of $-\dfrac{1}{3}$; two u quarks and one d quark (Table NP7). The neutron is neutral and can only be made from one charge of $+\dfrac{2}{3}$ and two charges of $-\dfrac{1}{3}$; one u and two d quarks.

Flavour

You can see that there are six different types of quark: up, down, strange, charm, bottom (or beauty) and top (or truth). Using this same colourful language, the properties of the quarks that enable them to be split up like this is called their *flavour*.

Different combinations of quarks

In the last few years, physicists have found evidence for different combinations of quarks. In 2002, Japanese physicists reported evidence for a particle with five quarks. This particle had been predicted by the Russian physicist, Diakonov, in 1997. This observation of a pentaquark was also reported by a US team in 2003.

In April 2003, physicists at the BaBar experiment in Stanford, USA reported evidence for a D-meson that might contain four quarks, but this evidence has not been confirmed.

In July 2003, physicists in Brookhaven, USA reported that they might have produced a state of matter in which quarks are not confined inside other particles; but again these observations have not been confirmed.

Fundamental forces

Leptons and quarks interact (influence each other) in four different ways, called the weak, electromagnetic, strong and gravitational interactions. These occur because of the fundamental properties of each type of particle, such as its mass or charge (Table NP9).

Table NP9 *The interactions felt by leptons and quarks*

Interaction	Leptons		Quarks
	Neutrinos	Charged leptons	
weak	✓	✓	✓
electromagnetic		✓	✓
strong			✓
gravitational	?	✓	✓

In an interaction, the particles are either *attracted towards* or *repelled away* from each other. Imagine that each particle and hadron is surrounded by a tiny field for each interaction in which it takes part.

Any quark has all four fields, whereas a neutrino is thought to have only one – the weak field. Particles interact only if they come close enough together for similar fields to overlap. If the field lines merge around both particles, they are pulled together. But if the lines do not merge, the particles are pushed apart (Figure NP13). These tiny pulls or pushes between particles are the origin of all the forces between large objects.

Exchange particles

During interactions, the energy associated with the field that causes the interaction can change. Sometimes the energy of the field decreases and another particle is formed. Sometimes a particle disappears and the energy of the field increases. So, the number and type of particles present can change. On this scale, energy can be exchanged only in fixed amounts, called *quanta*, just as light energy is packaged into quanta or particles called *photons*. The quanta are called *exchange particles*, to distinguish them from *matter particles*. Each field has its own type of exchange particle (Table NP10).

Interactions occur when particles come close enough for a quantum of energy to form and for an exchange to take place. The weak field is limited to about 10^{-18} m, well within the diameter of a hadron. In effect, the particles have to be in contact before this interaction can occur. The very short range is explained by the high mass of the W^+, W^- and Z^0 exchange particles. They require a lot of energy for their production and they decay very quickly into particles with lower mass. They have only a very short time and range in which to act.

(a) Attraction, e.g. strong force between quarks

(b) Repulsion, e.g. electromagnetic force between positive charges

(c) No interaction, e.g. a neutrino ignoring an electron. The weak fields do not come close enough to interact

Figure NP13 Particle interactions represented as fields.

Rutherford scattering shows that the electromagnetic field has a much greater range than the weak field or the strong field. Photons have no mass and so are easy to produce, and charged particles usually interact electromagnetically before the other fields are able to interact. Gluons also have zero mass, but have a short range because they themselves feel the strong field and cannot separate from quarks. The masses of individual particles are so small that gravitational interactions can be ignored. Mass nevertheless plays an important part in determining how the other three fields interact and exchange energy.

Table NP10 *Exchange particles*

Interaction	Name and symbol	Mass	Range	Typical decay times
weak	W^+, W^-, Z^0	~90 GeV	well within hadron	10^{-10} s
electromagnetic	photon γ	0	infinite	10^{-18} s
strong	gluon g	0	within hadron	10^{-23} s
gravitational	graviton *g*	0	infinite	–

NUCLEAR AND PARTICLE PHYSICS

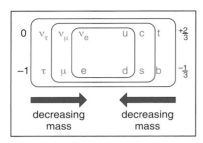

Figure NP14 The three generations of particles and their charges: antiparticles have the opposite charge.

Conservation laws

Interactions are related to the mass, the charge and the generation to which particles belong (Figure NP14). They obey specific conservation laws.

Mass-energy always has the same value before and after an interaction. Momentum and charge, Q, are also always conserved. The number of leptons, L, is also conserved. The appearance or disappearance of each lepton particle ($L = +1$) is always balanced by the appearance or disappearance of a lepton antiparticle ($L = -1$), even within each lepton generation.

The number of quarks is conserved, but quarks can be counted only in mesons ($q\bar{q}$) and baryons (qqq and $\bar{q}\bar{q}\bar{q}$). Mesons already balance a quark with an antiquark, and so can appear or disappear in interactions and are not conserved. By contrast, baryon number, B, is always conserved. There is the same balance between any baryons ($B = +1$) and antibaryons ($B = -1$) before and after every event.

Conservation of charm and strangeness

The weak interaction allows one type of quark to change into another. But in the other interactions, each type of quark is conserved; this applies particularly to charm, C, and strangeness, S. There is the same balance between c quarks ($C = +1$) and $\bar{c}$ quarks ($C = -1$) before and after an event. The same applies to strangeness, except that for s quarks $S = -1$ and for $\bar{s}$ quarks $S = +1$. For example, the D^+ meson in Table NP7 has $C = +1$, and the $\bar{\Lambda}$ antibaryon has $S = +1$. Although the $s\bar{s}$ meson is a strange particle, it has strangeness $S = 0$ because -1 balances $+1$, and also $C = 0$ as it has no c or $\bar{c}$ quarks.

Conservation laws can be used to check whether a particular interaction can or cannot occur, and to predict the properties of the products. Check how the laws apply in all the following interactions.

Weak interactions (W^+, W^- or Z^0 exchange)

These enable all lepton and quark particles and antiparticles to interchange energy, mass and charge, and so change from one into another, especially in decay processes. It is the only interaction felt by neutrinos, and since β^- decay involves a neutrino, it must involve the weak interaction. Look again at β^- and β^+ decay in terms of fundamental particles and the way they are conserved, especially the leptons.

For β^-:

	udd (neutron)	=	uud (proton)	+	e^-	+	$\bar{\nu}_e$
Q	$\left(+\dfrac{2}{3}-\dfrac{1}{3}-\dfrac{1}{3}\right)$	=	$\left(+\dfrac{2}{3}+\dfrac{2}{3}-\dfrac{1}{3}\right)$	+	(-1)	+	0
L	0	=	0	+	$(+1)$	+	(-1)
B	$(+1)$	=	$(+1)$	+	0	+	0

For β^+:

	uud (proton)	=	udd (neutron)	+	e^+	+	ν_e
Q	$\left(+\dfrac{2}{3}+\dfrac{2}{3}-\dfrac{1}{3}\right)$	=	$\left(+\dfrac{2}{3}-\dfrac{1}{3}-\dfrac{1}{3}\right)$	+	$(+1)$	+	0
L	0	=	0	+	(-1)	+	$(+1)$
B	$(+1)$	=	$(+1)$	+	0	+	0

In both cases, one type of quark changes into another, and a charged lepton and a neutrino from the same generation are produced. Simple sketches, called *Feynman diagrams*, show these events and how the different types of matter particle in Figure NP14 are related to each other by a weak exchange particle. The Feynman diagrams for β⁻ and β⁺ decay are shown in Figure NP15.

Weak decay processes occur naturally and the change is always to a particle of lower mass. This is why only particles of the first generation are abundant today. Check this and all the conservation laws for the Feynman diagrams in Figure NP16.

Particles of higher mass can appear if energy is available, as in collisions. This also happens in β⁺ decay, where a u quark acquires energy from the rest of the nucleus to change into a slightly more massive d (Figure NP15b).

The Z⁰ can also be involved in interactions between any of the particles, but it transfers only energy and mass, not charge. In some cases the particles simply scatter off each other. But if e⁺ and e⁻ are collided with sufficient energy, they momentarily become a Z⁰, which can then decay into a more massive pair of particles such as a μ⁻ and μ⁺. In some circumstances it is possible to deduce that a high-energy neutrino has collided with a proton and caused it to disintegrate into several hadrons (Figure NP17).

Electromagnetic interactions (photon exchange)

Electromagnetic forces are long-range attractions or repulsions between any particles or antiparticles that have a positive or negative electric charge. The only energy involved is the exchange of a photon, so both types of interaction are represented by the same Feynman diagram (Figure NP18). If the particles are attracted, like a proton and an electron, they remain together because there is a continual exchange of photons.

Matter–antimatter interactions

If particles of matter and antimatter come into contact, they destroy each other in a process called annihilation. This produces two identical, or occasionally three, photons, with the same total mass, energy and momentum as the original particles. Each photon can then materialise into new particles. All conservation laws are observed, because a particle–antiparticle pair is always materialised (e.g., μ⁻ and μ⁺, or d and d̄), so the conserved quantities must balance because they are equal and opposite (Figure NP18c).

A pair of leptons parts in opposite directions. But a quark pair is usually immediately bound together by the strong force and appears as one or more hadrons. The products vary according to the energy of the colliding particles.

Ring accelerators are used to collide beams of e⁺ and e⁻ or p and p̄ at different energies. The combined rest-mass energy of the e⁺ and e⁻ is 2×0.511 MeV = 1.02 MeV. If kinetic energy is increased, the collisions can reach 212 MeV, and it becomes possible to materialise a μ⁻ and μ⁺ pair; or, at 3.56 GeV, a τ⁻ and τ⁺ pair. This is how the tau was discovered. These

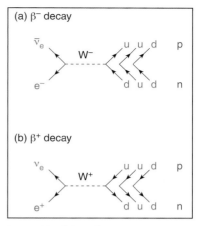

Figure NP15 Simple Feynman diagrams for β⁻ and β⁺ decay.

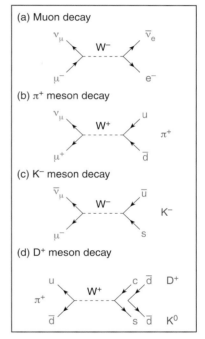

Figure NP16 Simple Feynman diagrams for weak interaction decays.

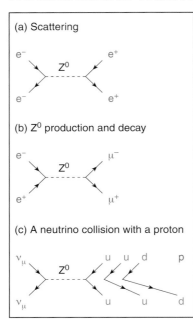

Figure NP17 Weak interactions involving the Z^0.

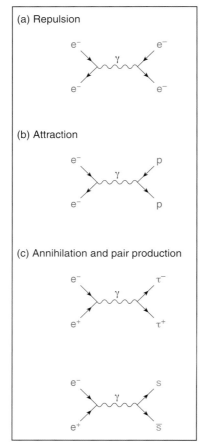

Figure NP18 Electromagnetic interactions.

massive leptons then decay separately into less massive particles and neutrinos, in a way similar to muon decay (Figure NP16a).

Mesons with zero charge can materialise at energies appropriate to their masses. The π^0 appears at energies above 0.135 GeV, $s\bar{s}$ at 0.958 GeV, $c\bar{c}$ at about 3 GeV and $b\bar{b}$ at about 10 GeV. Like all mesons, these are unstable and the quark and anti-quark annihilate into photons.

Annihilations of p and $\bar{p}$ give similar pair production, but because the rest-mass energy is so much higher, the number of pairs or the masses of the particles produced can be correspondingly greater.

Detecting neutrinos

Neutrinos can only interact with other particles if they collide with sufficient energy to form a W or Z exchange particle. In principle, neutrinos might be detected by making β^- decay go backwards, turning a proton into a neutron. But it is difficult to imagine how to make the $\bar{\nu}_e$, e^- and u quark collide at the same instant to make a d quark (Figure NP15a). However, the weak interaction actually changes leptons and quarks from one type to another, and the Feynman diagram suggests a different mechanism for detecting neutrinos. An incoming $\bar{\nu}_e$ could interact with a u quark in a proton and change to a e^+ as the u changes to a d quark (Figure NP19). Q, L and B are all conserved.

A suitable experiment could be designed only when the decays of the fission fragments in nuclear reactors created very large numbers of neutrinos:

A large tank of cadmium chloride solution was surrounded by 90 light detectors. Every few minutes, a $\bar{\nu}_e$ interacted with a u quark in the proton of a water molecule. The e^+ immediately annihilated with an e^- into a pair of photons, which travelled in opposite directions (conservation of momentum) and therefore caused flashes on opposite sides of the tank. The resulting neutron was free to scatter off other nuclei until it could be absorbed by one of the cadmium nuclei. This then emitted a burst of gamma rays to get rid of the excess energy. So two opposing flashes followed quickly by a burst of photons was very good evidence that $\bar{\nu}_e$ capture had occurred, especially as the frequency of the events could be related directly to the activity of the reactor core.

Strong interactions (gluon exchange)

Strong interactions are short-range attractions between all of the quarks and antiquarks. Leptons and antileptons are never involved. Quarks and antiquarks are strongly bound into mesons and baryons, from which they cannot separate, whereas the leptons are always observed as separate particles. Protons and neutrons are less strongly bound together in the nucleus by the residual effects of gluon exchange within the baryons themselves. This is the strong nuclear force.

The attraction between quarks can be represented by a Feynman diagram (Figure NP20a), but it is more interesting to look at interactions between the hadrons. Colliding protons may just scatter electromagnetically, but at higher energy new particles such as a π^0 ($d\bar{d}$) meson may materialise (Figure NP20b).

This and other strong interactions can be explained by imagining that a quark is displaced from one of the colliding protons. As it moves away from the others, the gluons have to travel over a longer distance. Unlike photons, the gluons themselves interact with the field, and at a range of about 10^{-15} m they materialise into a $q\bar{q}$ pair. All of the quarks then recombine into baryons and mesons.

If a charged meson appears, charge is conserved because one proton is replaced by a baryon with zero charge such as a neutron (Figure NP20c). As before, a d and $\bar{d}$ pair has materialised, but the quarks have combined in a different way, $u\bar{d}$ and dud instead of $d\bar{d}$ and uud. At even higher energy it is possible for more massive quarks from other generations to materialise (Figure NP20d). Check that Q, B and S are conserved. Strangeness and charm are always conserved in strong interactions because the quarks materialise in $q\bar{q}$ pairs.

At very high energies, more than one quark might be knocked a very long way from the others and a string of $q\bar{q}$ pairs can materialise along its path. These may combine to form various baryons, antibaryons and mesons. Some pairs might annihilate, but since quarks are always materialised or annihilated in pairs of similar type, the overall number of quarks of each type is always conserved in strong interactions.

Grand unification theories

Physicists are always looking for simple theories that cover a wide range of situations. In the case of forces, some have suggested that the gravitational force is caused by an exchange particle called the graviton. This might lead to a theory that describes all four different types of force.

The Z^0 acts on all particles and the photon only on charged particles, but otherwise they have very similar effects in some interactions. In mathematical terms, they appear to be alternative versions of the same particle, one with mass and one without. This has led to the idea that, at very high energies, it might also be possible to consider the gluon and maybe the graviton to be alternative versions of these particles, so leading to the idea of a single underlying field that would account for all known interactions and forces between matter.

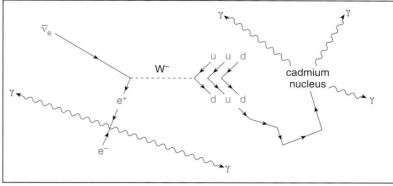

Figure NP19 Capture of an energetic neutrino.

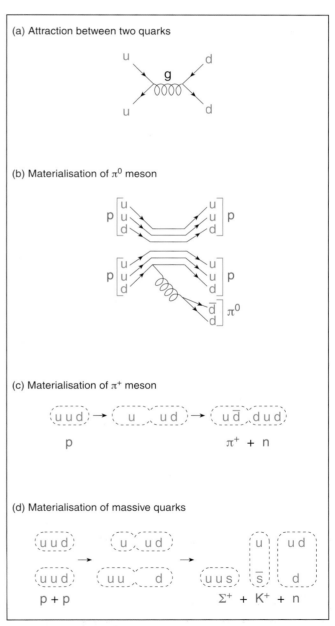

Figure NP20 Strong interactions.

Medical Physics

In this option you will find out how physics can be used to help people when they are ill. Medical physics can help in two broad ways – for **diagnosis** (finding out what is wrong) and **therapy** (making things better). Both diagnosis and therapy are about physical differences. If you want to find out what is wrong with someone, you need to find the difference between good and bad tissue, between a broken bone and a solid bone, between cancerous tissue and normal tissue. If you want to treat someone with cancer, you need a treatment that will kill cancerous tissue, but leaves the healthy tissue alone.

This section considers the uses of radionuclides, X-rays and ultrasound in medicine.

Nuclear medicine

In *Mechanics and Radioactivity*, you learned about radioactive nuclei – radionuclides. These emit alpha, beta and gamma radiation. These are types of *ionising radiation*. They are able to ionise (remove electrons from) other atoms and molecules. This can change the chemistry of cells in a living organism.

How does radiation affect living cells?

Kills cells: When radiation ionises an atom or molecule in a cell, very often the cell is not affected. When the cell is affected, the radiation usually kills the cell. So irradiating cells with alpha, beta or gamma radiation can kill the cells. Radioactivity, especially gamma radiation, is often used to kill cells. For example, when food is irradiated, the living organisms in it are killed (organisms that would make the food decompose faster), so it keeps longer on the shelves of our supermarkets. Also, doctors use ionising radiation to treat cancer, by using it to kill cancerous cells.

Mutates cells: Sometimes, radiation causes cells to change (*mutate*) so that they multiply abnormally quickly. They become cancerous cells that grow rapidly and spread disease throughout the body. The chances of getting cancer from radiation increase with the amount of radiation you receive.

Using gamma radiation for radiomedicine

Radionuclides can emit alpha, beta or gamma radiation. But most radiomedicine uses gamma radiation. Both alpha and beta radiation are easy to stop. Alpha radiation is stopped by the skin and beta radiation by a few centimetres of flesh. Gamma radiation can penetrate further. So the majority of radiomedicine uses gamma radiation.

Using gamma radiation for therapy

If a patient has cancer, one treatment is to kill cancerous tissue with ionising radiation. This is called *radiotherapy*. The element cobalt-60 emits gamma radiation that can be used for radiotherapy.

Figure M1 shows a cobalt-60 source being used to treat a cancer patient. The cobalt is enclosed in the large lead casing. Lead plates shield as much as possible of the patient's healthy tissue from the source, while the gamma radiation kills the cancerous tissue. You can read more about radiotherapy later in this Option.

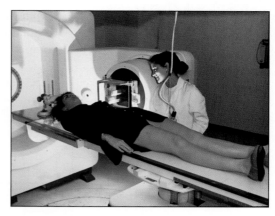

Figure M1 Cobalt-60 source being used to treat a patient.

Using gamma radiation for diagnosis

Radioisotopes can be used for diagnosis, as well. A radiologist injects a radionuclide into the body. This decays and emits gamma radiation that can be detected with a gamma camera, to follow the path of the radionuclide through the patient's body.

The radiographer chooses a chemical compound, containing a gamma emitter, that will be absorbed by the part of the body under investigation. For example, one isotope of technetium ($^{99m}_{43}$Tc) gives out gamma radiation. Technetium can be made into many different compounds to be absorbed by the brain, lungs, liver, bone, heart and circulatory system. The gamma emissions for these organs can be used to study their functions.

Radioactive isotopes of iodine can be taken by mouth. They travel through the bloodstream and are absorbed by the thyroid gland. Radiologists can then measure the emissions from the thyroid gland. When they have made many measurements from many different thyroids, they know how a healthy or model thyroid behaves. They compare the thyroid emissions from a particular patient with those from a model thyroid, to see if the patient's thyroid is normal.

Dilution radiology

If you have a serious accident and have lost a lot of blood, the doctors will want to know how much you have lost. Radiographers can use radioisotopes to measure the amount of blood in your body, in order to find out how much more is needed.

The radiologist first injects the patient with a known volume of radioactive tracer, with a known activity. Perhaps they would inject 10 cm^3 of saline with an activity of 250 000 Bq. After a few minutes, they take a sample of the same volume of blood from the patient and measure its activity.

If, for example, the activity had dropped to 500 Bq, this is $\dfrac{500 \text{ Bq}}{250\,000 \text{ Bq}} = \dfrac{1}{500}$

of the original activity. The activity has been diluted 500 times, so the volume of the saline has been diluted 500 times. So the volume of blood in the patient must be 500 × 10 cm^3 = 5000 cm^3 = 5 litres.

The gamma camera

Radiologists use gamma cameras to form an image of gamma emissions from within the body (Figure M2). The gamma camera consists of four parts: a collimator, a sodium iodide scintillator, a set of photomultiplier tubes and a computer processor.

Here's how it works:

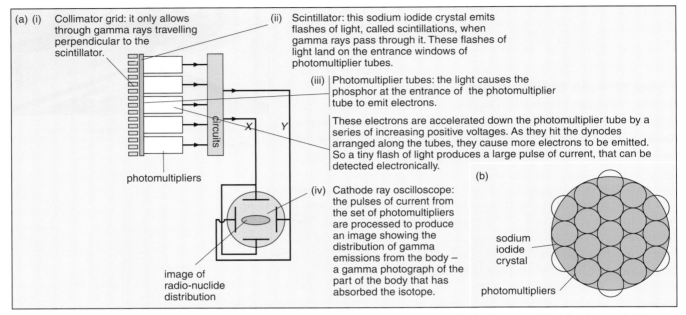

(a) (i) Collimator grid: it only allows through gamma rays travelling perpendicular to the scintillator.

(ii) Scintillator: this sodium iodide crystal emits flashes of light, called scintillations, when gamma rays pass through it. These flashes of light land on the entrance windows of photomultiplier tubes.

(iii) Photomultiplier tubes: the light causes the phosphor at the entrance of the photomultiplier tube to emit electrons.

These electrons are accelerated down the photomultiplier tube by a series of increasing positive voltages. As they hit the dynodes arranged along the tubes, they cause more electrons to be emitted. So a tiny flash of light produces a large pulse of current, that can be detected electronically.

photomultipliers

(iv) Cathode ray oscilloscope: the pulses of current from the set of photomultipliers are processed to produce an image showing the distribution of gamma emissions from the body – a gamma photograph of the part of the body that has absorbed the isotope.

image of radio-nuclide distribution

(b)

sodium iodide crystal

photomultipliers

Figure M2 The gamma camera. (a) Gamma radiation produces flashes of light in the crystal, which are amplified by photomultipliers and processed by the circuits. (b) Arrangement of photomultiplier tubes.

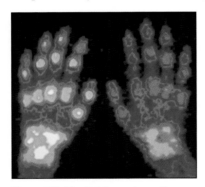

Figure M3 The bright spots on the left hand show the concentration of the radionuclide, produced by inflamed joints.

Figure M3 shows a gamma camera image of hands with inflamed joints (arthritis). The left hand has severe arthritis and the radionuclide has concentrated in the joints of this hand.

Radioactive and biological half-life

You already know that the radioactive half-life of an isotope is the average time it takes for one-half of the nuclei in a sample to decay. When a radioisotope is introduced into the body this decay process continues, reducing the amount of radioisotope in the body. At the same time, the body processes the radioisotope, eventually passing it out of the body. The average time for an organ to excrete one-half of a sample is called the *biological half-life*. Both radioactive half-life t_r and biological half-life t_b reduce the amount of a radionuclide remaining in the body. The effective half-life t_e takes into account both factors:

$$\frac{1}{t_e} = \frac{1}{t_r} + \frac{1}{t_b}$$

For example, the radioactive half-life of iodine-131 is 8 days. Its biological half-life is 21 days. You can calculate the effective half-life:

$$\frac{1}{t_e} = \frac{1}{t_r} + \frac{1}{t_b}$$

$$\frac{1}{t_e} = \frac{1}{8} + \frac{1}{21} = 0.125 + 0.048 = 0.173$$

$$\therefore t_e = 5.8 \text{ days.}$$

Radiographers choose their radiochemicals with half-lives that are appropriate to the experiments they are carrying out. They want a half-life which ensures that the isotopes are present and active during the investigation.

Radiological protection
Any exposure of the body to radioactive emissions carries some risk. For this reason, radioactivity is used only when the possible benefits are greater than the risks.

Radiographers choose radionuclides with effective half-lives as short as possible, compatible with the time needed for the experiment. This minimises the patients' exposure to radiation. They generally avoid radioisotopes that emit alpha and beta radiation (because these kill or damage cells without leaving the body and so are no use for imaging). They prefer radioisotopes that emit gamma radiation, only.

For instance, there are two radioactive isotopes of iodine. ^{131}I emits both gamma and beta radiation. You can use its gamma radiation to trace its movement throughout the body. But the beta emission it releases can kill or damage healthy cells.

Nowadays, ^{123}I is used in preference to ^{131}I for testing thyroid function, because it is a pure gamma emitter, and has no alpha or beta emissions to give an unnecessary dose of radiation to the body.

On the other hand, patients with an over-active thyroid take doses of ^{131}I so that the beta radiation emitted destroys part of the thyroid and reduces its activity.

Radiographers protect themselves with lead shielding to minimise the doses they receive.

Producing radionuclides for use in nuclear medicine
Most radionuclides used in medicine are prepared by neutron bombardment in a nuclear reactor. Iodine-131 (^{131}I) is an example of a radionuclide produced in this way. Tellurium-130 (^{130}Te) is placed in a nuclear reactor and, under the intense bombardment, eventually captures a neutron. The resulting nuclide then decays to ^{131}I by emission of beta radiation as the equation shows:

$$^{130}_{52}\text{Te} + ^{1}_{0}\text{n} \rightarrow ^{131}_{52}\text{Te} \rightarrow ^{131}_{53}\text{I} + ^{0}_{-1}\beta$$

^{131}I has a half-life of about 8 days. It emits a beta-minus (β^-) particle and some gamma radiation:

$$^{131}_{53}\text{I} \rightarrow ^{131}_{54}\text{Xe} + ^{0}_{-1}\beta + \gamma$$

$^{99}_{42}$Mo, a widely used molybdenum radionuclide, is also produced by neutron bombardment. $^{99}_{42}$Mo has a half-life of 67 hours and decays to a nuclide of technetium:

$$^{99}_{42}\text{Mo} \rightarrow ^{99m}_{43}\text{Tc} + ^{0}_{-1}\beta$$

MEDICAL PHYSICS

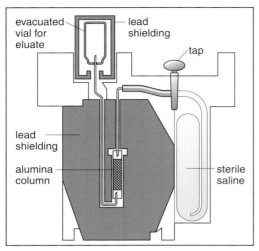

Figure M4 Saline solution, drawn through the alumina column by the vacuum in the vial, dissolves technetium.

The 'm' in $^{99m}_{43}$Tc means that the technetium is metastable (the nucleus is in a higher energy state than normal). It decays down to stable $^{99}_{43}$Tc by emitting a gamma ray. The half-life for this decay is 6.0 hours. For the medical physicist, the important part of this decay is the emission of gamma radiation, which can be detected.

Elution

A radiographer needs a handy source of a convenient gamma emitter. One such source is a technetium generator called an *elution cell*. Figure M4 shows an elution cell. The alumina (a naturally occurring compound of aluminium oxide) column holds the chemicals. It contains a molybdenum compound, made with $^{99}_{42}$Mo. This decays continuously, producing a compound of $^{99m}_{43}$Tc. When the technetium is required, saline (salt) solution is passed through the alumina column and dissolves the technetium compound, but not the insoluble molybdenum. The eluted technetium solution is collected in the glass container.

X-rays

X-rays are part of the electromagnetic spectrum. They are high-frequency, short-wavelength electromagnetic waves. X-rays are used for both diagnosis and therapy.

Figure M5 shows a typical X-ray tube. The low-voltage supply provides a current that heats the filament. This gets hot enough to emit electrons. The high-voltage supply makes the anode very positive, with respect to the filament, and attracts the emitted electrons. The electrons hit the anode at high speed, giving up their kinetic energy.

The design of the X-ray tube ensures that the electrons hit a small area on the anode. This area is the source of all the X-rays, which then spread out over a range of directions.

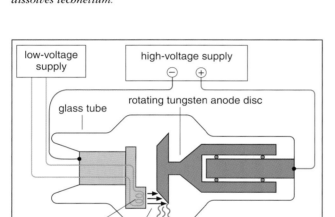

Figure M5 When electrons hit the anode, they give out X-rays.

The energy of X-rays

The energy of X-rays is measured in electronvolts (eV). One electronvolt = 1.6×10^{-19} J. If the voltage between the anode and cathode in an X-ray tube is 70 kV, the kinetic energy of an electron just before it hits the anode is 70 keV. If this electron gives up all its kinetic energy as X-rays, the maximum energy of X-rays emitted is 70 keV.

Most electrons give up only a proportion of their energy as X-ray photons. So the tube produces a range of X-ray energies, called a *spectrum*, with a maximum energy determined by the voltage between the anode and cathode.

In fact, most of the kinetic energy of the electrons ends up increasing the temperature of the anode. For some X-ray tubes, less than 1% of the electrons' kinetic energy is released as X-rays. The efficiency of the tube is less than 1%. This is why the anode is made to spin, so the target area can cool down briefly during each revolution.

Low- and high-voltage X-rays

Radiographers generally use two broad ranges of X-rays – those with energies of around 100 keV, and those with energies of around 1 MeV. The difference in properties between the two different types of X-rays makes each suitable for different purposes.

The inverse square law

X-rays spread out. As Figure M6 shows, the further away the source is, the more area the X-rays cover. This means that the *intensity* of the X-rays (the amount of power per unit area) is less. If you double the distance from the source, the area covered by the X-rays multiplies by four, and the intensity decreases to one-quarter. If you treble the distance, the intensity decreases to one-ninth. This is the *inverse square law*.

The intensity of X-rays is inversely proportional to the square of the distance from the source.

$$\text{Intensity} \propto \frac{1}{r^2}$$

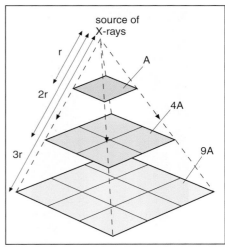

Figure M6 *The area covered by the X-rays is proportional to the square of the distance from the source.*

X-rays for diagnosis

Figure M7a shows how a radiograph is produced with X-rays. The tube emits X-rays, which pass through the patient's body and strike the photographic film.

The image on the film is called a *radiograph*. It is the shadow of any object placed between it and the X-ray source. A point source of X-rays produces shadows with sharp edges. As Figure M7b shows, if the source of X-rays is wide, the shadow is fuzzy. You can see these effects for yourself by using a light bulb, instead of the X-ray tube, and a piece of card with a small hole in it.

When X-rays hit the photographic plate, they darken the plate. When the X-rays are strong, for instance where they have travelled through the air space inside the lungs, the radiograph is very dark. Where the X-rays pass through bones and are strongly absorbed, the radiograph is light.

Between the patient and the photographic plate is a lead *anti-scatter grid* (Figure M8). This works like the collimator in the gamma camera. It allows through only X-rays that have come directly to the plate and stops X-rays that have been scattered by the patient's body hitting the plate. Scattered X-rays hitting the plate would confuse the image and reduce its sharpness.

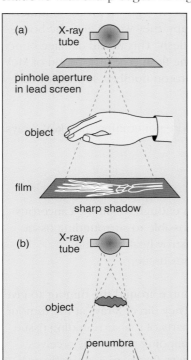

Figure M7 *To get sharp X-ray photographs, you need a point source.*

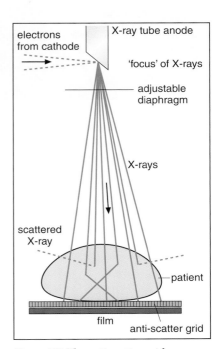

Figure M8 *The anti-scatter grid enhances the clarity of the X-ray by preventing scattered X-rays from hitting the photographic plate.*

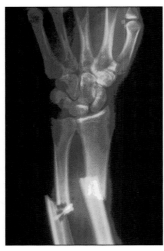

Figure M9 X-rays with energy in the order of 100 keV produce sharp shadows of bones.

X-rays with energies of around 100 keV are used for diagnosis. For X-rays with this energy, absorption is strongly dependent on the proton number of the elements through which they are travelling. So atoms with a large proton number absorb much more strongly. Calcium in bones (proton number 20) absorbs much more than the hydrogen ($Z = 1$) or oxygen ($Z = 8$) in the water of soft tissues. So bones cause dark shadows on X-ray films (Figure M9).

X-rays for therapy

Both X-rays and gamma rays are electromagnetic waves. The only difference between them is that X-rays are produced by stopping electrons and gamma rays are produced by nuclear decay. So X-rays can be used for therapy (such as killing cancerous tissue), just like gamma rays. You can compare X-rays with gamma rays if you use electronvolts to measure the energy of the two types of rays.

The gamma rays from a cobalt-60 source have energies of about 1.3 MeV. This is very much higher than the energies of X-rays used for diagnosis. In fact, this higher energy is useful in therapy, so X-rays for therapy generally have energies in the order of megaelectronvolts.

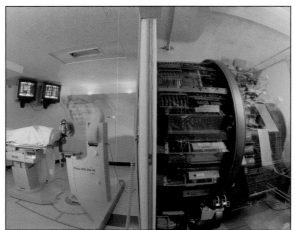

Figure M10 This linac, hidden behind a wall in the treatment room, produces X-rays with energies of many megaelectronvolts.

Conventional X-ray tubes can produce X-rays up to a few hundred keV. To produce MeV X-rays, hospitals use a device called a *linac* (linear accelerator). A linac produces X-rays with energies one thousand times larger than a conventional X-ray tube – up to several hundred megaelectronvolts (Figure M10).

MeV X-rays have two advantages for therapy. You know that the absorption of keV X-rays depends strongly on proton number. If keV X-rays were used for therapy, they would give the bones a much stronger dose than the flesh. This would damage bone, while under-treating cancer in the flesh. The absorption of MeV X-rays is not so dependent on proton number, so that it does not unduly damage bone.

The second advantage is that MeV X-rays are more penetrating than keV X-rays. They can treat cancer deep inside the body.

Planning X-ray treatment

For X-ray therapy, you want the dose to be high enough to kill the cancerous tissue, but you want to do as little damage as possible to surrounding tissue. The dose is therefore critical. Too much will destroy healthy tissue unnecessarily; too little will not kill the cancerous tissue.

Radiographers rotate the X-ray or gamma ray source around the tumour to give treatments with multiple beams (Figure M11). They direct X-rays at the tumour from a range of angles, each through different parts of the surrounding tissue. The tumour gets exposed all the time: the surrounding tissue only receives certain beams. The radiographer uses an alignment device to aim the beams accurately at the tumour, first marking the beam entry points permanently on the patient's skin. Sometimes a 'mask' is used, which is specially made to fit the patient and keep him/her still to ensure that the beam hits the required area.

Much X-ray treatment of cancer is *palliative* – it provides relief from the effects of the cancer, but does not completely cure it.

Ultrasound

Another type of wave is very useful in medicine. Sound waves are mechanical, not electromagnetic. They are longitudinal vibrations in a medium. You can hear frequencies up to about 20 kHz, but sound waves of much higher frequencies, called ultrasound, can be produced.

Ultrasound for diagnosis

Ultrasound is a useful medical tool for exploring the body. It is commonly used to monitor the growth, development and general health of a baby in its mother's womb. It is also used to examine the health of soft-tissue organs, such as the bladder.

Medical ultrasonics uses a probe to send out pulses of ultrasound and receives the echoes from each boundary (Fig. M12). This is the sonar principle – the same system bats use for navigation.

Ultrasound for therapy

Ultrasound is also used to treat certain medical conditions. It can help some types of sore tissue to heal rapidly, and can also destroy gallstones and kidney stones.

Specific acoustic impedance

Medical ultrasonics relies on a property called the specific acoustic impedance Z. This is found by multiplying the speed of sound in a medium, c by the density of the medium ρ.

$$Z = c\rho$$

If ultrasound arrives at a boundary between two materials with different specific acoustic impedances, some ultrasound is reflected at the boundary. These reflections are analysed and give information about the structure of the body. The specific acoustic impedances for various materials are shown in Table M1.

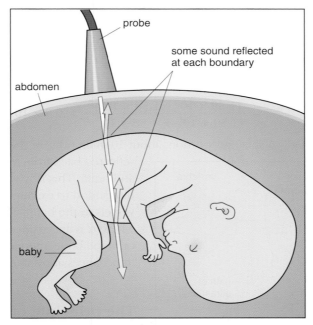

Figure M12 Ultrasound is used to monitor the development of a baby in its mother's womb: the probe sends out ultrasound waves that reflect from each boundary.

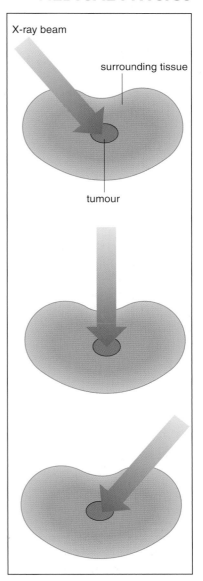

Figure M11 The tumour receives a continuous dose of radiation – the healthy tissue receives only some of the radiation.

Table M1 *Some specific acoustic impedances*

Medium	Specific acoustic impedance /kg m^{-2} s^{-1}
Air	0.000439×10^6
Fat	1.38×10^6
Water	1.50×10^6
Brain	1.58×10^6
Blood	1.59×10^6
Muscle	$\sim 1.7 \times 10^6$
Bone	$\sim 6 \times 10^6$

Calculating the amount of sound reflected

On an ultrasound scan, the strength of the reflection at a boundary, and the brightness with which it shows up, depend on the specific acoustic impedances of the two media at the boundary. The ratio of the sound intensity reflected from the boundary (I_r) to the sound intensity incident on the boundary (I_i) is called the *intensity reflection coefficient* α. The value of α depends on Z_1 and Z_2, the specific acoustic impedances of the two media, and is calculated from:

$$\alpha = \frac{I_r}{I_i} = \frac{(Z_2 - Z_1)^2}{(Z_2 + Z_1)^2}$$

To calculate the proportion of the intensity reflected at a boundary (for instance, between blood and brain), you substitute values in the equation:

$$\alpha = \frac{I_r}{I_i} = \frac{(Z_2 - Z_1)^2}{(Z_2 + Z_1)^2}$$

$$= \frac{(1.59 \times 10^6 - 1.58 \times 10^6)^2}{(1.59 \times 10^6 + 1.58 \times 10^6)^2} = 9.9 \times 10^{-6}$$

Only a small proportion, about 10 millionths, of the sound intensity is reflected back from a boundary between blood and brain. This is why it is difficult to use ultrasound to examine the structure of the blood vessels in the brain. The strongest reflections, where α is approximately 1, come from air/bone or blood/bone interfaces, where the acoustic impedances are very different.

The principle of ultrasound scanning

A short pulse, with a frequency of the order of a few MHz, is applied to a transducer in a probe. This transmits a pulse of sound waves and then receives the reflections, as shown in Figure M13a. The layer of gel between the probe and the body is a *coupling medium*: it replaces the air layer, which would cause large reflections and would thus stop the ultrasound penetrating the body.

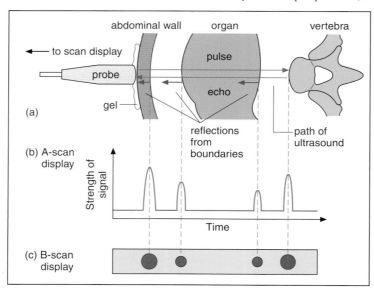

Figure M13 Reflections from boundaries can be displayed either as a graph (A-scan) or as spots of different brightness (B-scan).

Figure M13b shows an A-scan (amplitude scan), which is a graph of the strength of the reflected signal against time. From this graph, the radiographer can find the depth of the reflecting boundaries. A-scans are used to make precise measurements on the eye.

Figure M13c shows a B-scan (brightness scan). Compare it with the A-scan above. In the B-scan, the brightness of a spot of light on a display screen is proportional to the strength of the reflected signal.

Two-dimensional B-scans

A probe containing several transducers can sweep ultrasound pulses across an area of the body and produce individual B-scans at different angles. These can be assembled on the display to produce a cross-section of the part of the body being scanned. Figure M14 shows a scan of a 12-week-old baby in the uterus. The scans are repeated 25 times per second to produce a moving, real-time image of the area being scanned.

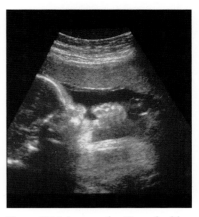

Figure M14 A scan of a 12-week-old baby in the uterus. The baby is sucking its thumb. Can you identify its hand and the individual fingers?

Figure M15 shows a block diagram of an ultrasound scanner.

The clock controls the whole system.

The time delay shows how deep the boundary is; the position controller decides which direction it is; and the receiver controls the brightness.

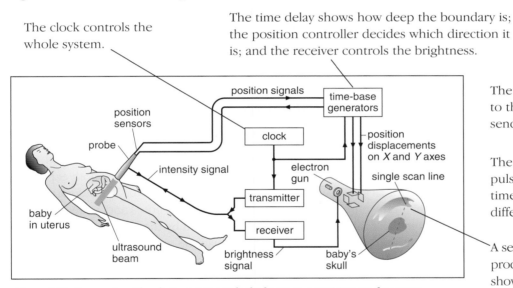

Figure M15 B-scanning. The electron gun sends the beam to a position on the screen corresponding with the source of the reflection. The brightness of the spot indicates the strength of reflection.

The **transmitter** sends signals to the probe, which causes it to send out a single pulse.

The **receiver** receives the pulse reflected at different times from different places at different intensities.

A sequence of reflections produces a line on the screen showing the boundary between two media.

The resolution of ultrasound

The speed of waves is related to the frequency and wavelength by the equation:

Speed = frequency × wavelength.

The speed of ultrasound in tissue is typically around 1500 m s^{-1}. So for a frequency of 2 MHz:

Speed = frequency × wavelength.

1500 m s^{-1} = 2 000 000 Hz × wavelength

$$\text{wavelength} = \frac{1500 \text{ m s}^{-1}}{2\ 000\ 000 \text{ Hz}} = 0.75 \text{ mm}$$

The wavelength limits the *resolution*, the smallest separation you can see. For good resolution (i.e. to see tiny details), you want short wavelength and therefore high frequency.

Ultrasound waves are absorbed by the tissue through which they pass. The higher the frequency, the greater the attenuation (weakening) of the signal. So, for good penetration, you want low frequency. The choice of frequency is therefore a compromise between resolution and penetration, leading to the use of frequencies between 2 MHz and 10 MHz.

Depth information comes from measuring the time between a pulse leaving the probe and returning. For good depth resolution, short pulses are needed. But short pulses contain less energy and are more easily absorbed. The choice of pulse length, like the choice of frequency, is a compromise between resolution and penetration.

Ultrasound compared with X-rays

Ultrasound imaging is safer than using X-rays. There are no known hazards connected with the low-power ultrasound used for scanning. But all X-rays have a chance of doing damage, whatever the dose. Both ultrasound and X-rays can produce real-time, two-dimensional images and they both expose the tissue for as long as observations are being made. Safety considerations mean that ultrasound is used routinely for these purposes and X-rays are used only when the comparatively high risk is justified by the benefits. For instance, if a patient is likely to die from cancer anyway, the extra dose of radiation will not be considered a great risk.

The penetration of ultrasound is limited, particularly where there are air/tissue or bone/tissue interfaces. So you cannot use ultrasound to investigate the chest cavity. But X-rays are poor at resolving soft tissues, so are not good for examining the organs of the abdomen. The wavelength of all X-rays is much less than the shortest ultrasound wavelength, so the resolution of X-ray equipment can be much better than the resolution of ultrasound equipment.

The slow speed of ultrasound and the fact that it reflects from tissue means that you can get depth information directly from an ultrasound scan. So ultrasound produces sectional maps of reflection. Tissue boundaries do not reflect X-rays and, even if they did, X-rays travel at the speed of light, so it would be difficult to measure the time delay. So to get depth information from X-rays you need to use *tomography* – taking several images from a range of angles to produce information about a cross-section. Ordinary X-ray radiographs are shadows – projection maps of transmission.

Practice questions

Chapter 1

1.1 What is an electric current?

1.2 In what way is electrical work being done in the circuit in Figure 1.1 in Chapter 1? How are electrical and mechanical work similar?

1.3 What is the difference between a cell and a battery?

1.4 Draw 'engine diagrams' for circuits A to D. Predict what will happen in each circuit. In which circuits will the engine run out of fuel fastest?

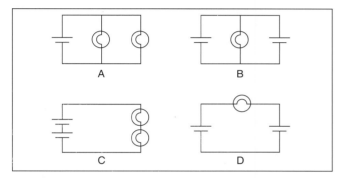

1.5 With reference to the movement of electrons, explain the difference between direct and alternating currents.

Chapter 2

2.1 Two objects, A and B, are initially uncharged. A negative charge of 4 nC flows from A to B. What is then the charge on each object?

2.2 Explain why a neutral acetate rod becomes positive when rubbed with a duster.

2.3 Charge and current are both physical quantities. Which is a base quantity and which is a derived quantity? State their units. What is the relationship between them?

2.4 Calculate the charge that flows when a current of (a) 3 A flows for 4 s, (b) 7 A flows for 8 minutes, (c) 0.25 A flows for 2 hours.

2.5 Find the current when a charge of (a) 700 C passes a point in 35 s, (b) 3600 C passes a point in 3 minutes.

2.6 A current of 4.5 A flows in a car headlamp bulb for 20 minutes. Calculate the total charge that passes through the filament. How many electrons pass a given point in the filament during this time?
[charge on 1 electron = 1.6×10^{-19} C]

2.7 Express the coulomb in terms of base units.

Chapter 3

3.1 What advice would you give to a student who was about to set up a circuit for the first time?

3.2 Explain how you would measure the current at a particular point in a circuit that had already been set up. How would you make sure that you didn't get a negative reading?

3.3 Give typical values for the current through the following components in normal operation: torch bulb, LED, small motor, buzzer, mains lamp, electric kettle.

3.4 What is a series circuit? Why should we expect the current at all points in a series circuit to be the same?

3.5 Electricity company A advertises that it charges its customers for the amount of current they use; company B for the amount of charge; company C for the amount of energy. Explain why company C will be the only one making any charges.

Chapter 4

4.1 What is a parallel circuit? What happens to the current as it flows into and out of a parallel circuit?

4.2 State Kirchhoff's first law. Which conservation law does Kirchhoff's first law relate to?

4.3 Three identical lamps are connected in parallel to a battery. Draw a circuit diagram of the arrangement. The current through one lamp is 800 mA. Mark on all wires on your diagram the value of the current in that wire.

4.4 You have to power four identical 3 V lamps. Draw circuit diagrams of them connected (a) in series to a 12 V battery (b) in parallel to a 3 V battery. For each circuit mark the currents in each wire.

PRACTICE QUESTIONS

4.5 Find the unknown currents I_1 to I_9 in the circuits A to D.

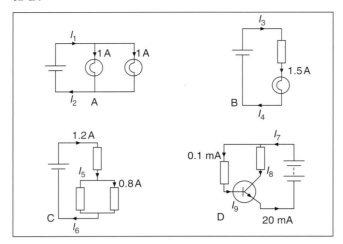

Chapter 5

5.1 What is the effect of adding a resistor in series with a circuit? Give four physical ways in which a circuit could be given additional resistance.

5.2 Design a circuit that uses an LDR to make a light meter.

5.3 Design a circuit that will switch on a warning lamp, which takes a small current, when the temperature of a sensor becomes too high.

5.4 An electric fire and a lamp are both connected to the mains supply. Draw a circuit diagram for this arrangement. The fire takes a current of 12 A and the lamp 0.4 A. Mark on your diagram the values of the currents in each wire.

5.5 Why is it not possible to use an LDR directly to enable a motor to start as the level of illumination increases? Explain how an LDR can be used with an electromagnetic relay to accomplish this task.

Chapter 6

6.1 What voltage results when three cells, each 1.5 V, are connected in series? When connected in parallel, these cells have a resulting voltage of 1.5 V. Is there any advantage in using these cells in parallel in place of a single cell?

6.2 When a steady current flows in a wire, the charge carriers (electrons) have a constant average drift speed despite being continually pushed along by the power supply. Explain why the electrons do not accelerate continually.

6.3 Copy the circuit diagram and show how you would use a voltmeter to measure all the voltages. Label the positive terminal of the voltmeter in each case.

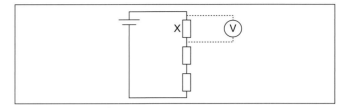

6.4 Calculate the unknown voltages.

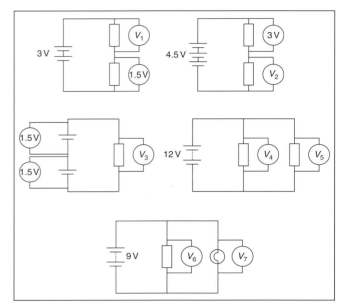

6.5 How do voltage differences across components that help charge move in a circuit differ from those across components that hinder this movement?

Chapter 7

7.1 Give two examples each of components that give energy to a circuit and those that take it away. State the names used to distinguish the voltage differences across these two groups of components.

7.2 How many joules of energy does a 9 V battery supply when (a) a charge of 15 C passes through it, (b) a current of 0.5 A flows through it for 2 minutes?

7.3 A heater supplies 36 000 J of energy in 10 minutes when a current of 3 A flows. (a) How much energy is produced each second? (b) How much charge passes through the heater each second? (c) How much energy is produced each time a coulomb passes through the heater?

7.4 The power of a torch bulb is 0.75 W when the current through it is 0.3 A. Calculate the potential difference across the bulb?

7.5 The energy transfer by a small generator was 0.3 MJ when driving a current of 2.5 A for 10 minutes. How much charge passes through the generator in this time? Calculate its electromotive force.

Chapter 8

8.1 A 12 V battery drives current through three 1 kΩ resistors in a series circuit. Draw a circuit diagram of this arrangement and mark on it sensible values for the voltages across each component. Mark the direction of current flow in each wire.

8.2 Repeat question 8.1 for the circuit with the three 1 kΩ resistors in parallel.

8.3 What are the unknown voltages, V_1 to V_5, in the circuits shown?

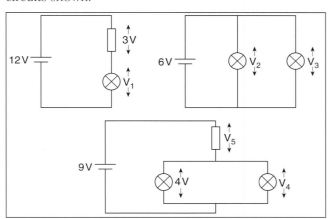

8.4 Figure 8.3 in Chapter 8 shows a water circuit, part of which includes a mountain with two streams flowing down it. Draw the circuit diagram of an equivalent electric circuit. Name the source of power in each circuit. How can the water circuit be used to illustrate Kirchhoff's first law?

8.5 Two identical resistance wires, AB and CD, are connected in parallel across a battery as shown. State

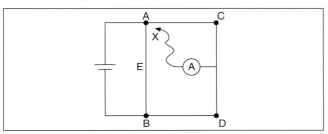

and explain what happens to the current flow through the ammeter as wire X is moved along the resistance wire from A to E to B.

Chapter 9

9.1 Explain the terms voltage at a point and voltage across a component.

9.2 The diagram shows a circuit with voltages marked at different points. Find the potential difference across (a) the lamp, (b) the resistor, (c) the wire connecting the lamp and the resistor.

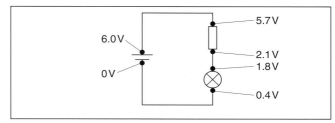

9.3 Sketch a voltage-position graph for the circuit in Question 9.2.

9.4 What are the unknown voltages, V_1 to V_{14}, in the circuits shown?

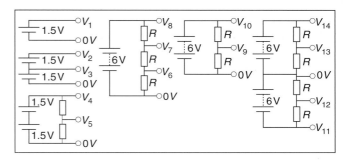

9.5 State Kirchhoff's second law.

9.6 Explain how Kirchhoff's second law is a direct consequence of energy conservation.

Chapter 10

10.1 Express the volt and the ohm in terms of only base units.

10.2 With the aid of a circuit diagram, explain how you would measure the resistance of a component. You do not have access to a digital ohmmeter.

10.3 The combined resistance of two resistors is 120 Ω. One of the resistors has a resistance of 180 Ω. Are the two resistors connected in series or in parallel? Calculate the resistance of the other resistor.

PRACTICE QUESTIONS

10.4 You are provided with three 18 Ω resistors which can be used individually, in pairs or in combinations involving all three. Sketch each of the seven possible resistor combinations and calculate the combined resistance in each case.

10.5 The resistance of the filament of an 810 mW torch bulb is 25 Ω. Calculate the current required for full brightness. How many 1.5 V cells would be needed to power this torch bulb?

Chapter 11

11.1 Explain (i) why an ideal voltmeter should have infinite resistance, (ii) why an ideal ammeter should have zero resistance.

11.2 Figures 11.1 and 11.2 in Chapter 11 show two circuits for measuring the voltage and current for a resistor. Explain why neither circuit produces correct values for both readings unless both measuring instruments are ideal. For each circuit, explain whether the value of resistance calculated from the readings will be higher or lower than the resistor's actual value.

11.3 Describe carefully how you would use a digital ohmmeter to measure a resistance.

11.4 Sketch graphs to show how resistance varies with temperature for (a) a coil of wire and (b) a negative-temperature-coefficient thermistor.

11.5 How does the resistance of a light-dependent resistor vary with the level of illumination falling on it?

Chapter 12

12.1 The diameter of a tennis ball is 66 mm. How many tennis balls will it take to fill a box with sides of 1 m if they are all stacked together in a cubic structure?

12.2 A copper connecting wire has a cross-sectional area of 3 mm^2 and is 30 cm long. Use information from Chapter 12 to help you estimate the amount of free charge in this wire. How long will it take for all this free charge to pass through the wire when a current of 3 A flows? Hence find the average speed at which this free charge moves.

12.3 Explain why your room light comes on at almost the same instant as you close its switch despite the very slow movement of the electrons in the wires connecting it to the mains supply.

12.4 A copper wire, as used for house mains wiring, has a cross-sectional area of 2.5 mm^2 and carries a maximum current of 25 A. The charge is carried by electrons, of which there are about 7.0×10^{28} per metre cubed. The charge on an electron is $(-)1.6 \times 10^{-19}$ C. Calculate the drift speed of the electrons when the wire carries its maximum current.

12.5 Describe how you would demonstrate the slow speed at which the current carriers move through a circuit.

Chapter 13

13.1 Define resistivity and state its unit. Express this unit in terms of only base units.

13.2 Explain why the tungsten filament of a lamp gets much hotter than its copper connecting wires.

13.3 A copper track on a printed circuit board is 2.0 mm wide, 8.5 mm thick and 4.0 cm long. Calculate its resistance. Find the voltage drop across it when it carries a current of 25 mA.

13.4 With reference to the equation $I = nAqv$, explain why the resistance of a tungsten filament lamp increases with increasing temperature whereas that of an NTC thermistor decreases.

13.5 An NTC thermistor at room temperature has a resistance of 300 Ω. Find the current that flows when it has a voltage of 12 V connected across it. How much power does this current generate as it flows through the thermistor? If the thermistor then gives out energy to its surroundings at a rate of 300 mW, what happens to (a) the thermistor's temperature, (b) its resistance? What effects will this change in resistance have on the current flowing and the power generated within the thermistor? What would be the likely outcome if this process were to continue?

13.6 For each of the following materials, state whether you would expect their resistivity to rise or fall as the temperature increases: copper, carbon, glass, iron, paraffin wax, silicon.

Chapter 14

14.1 State the function of a potential divider circuit.

14.2 Assuming that no current is being taken from its output, calculate the output voltage V_{OUT} of this potential divider.

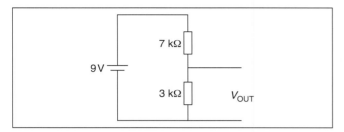

14.3 Predict what would happen to V_{OUT} in Question 14.2 if a current were taken from the output of the potential divider. Explain your reasoning.

14.4 For the following circuit, calculate (a) the combined resistance of the parallel combination, (b) the total circuit resistance, (c) the current supplied by the battery, (d) the potential difference across the 360 Ω resistor, (e) the potential difference across the parallel combination, (f) the current flowing through the 600 Ω resistor, (g) the current flowing through the 400 Ω resistor.

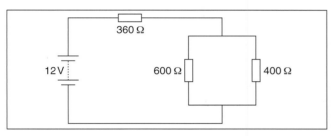

14.5 For the following circuit, calculate the current through each resistor.

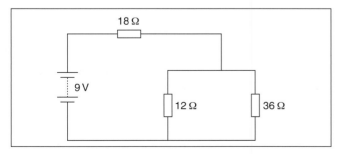

Chapter 15

15.1 The brightness of a lamp can be controlled using either a rheostat or a potentiometer. Compare the ways in which these two devices work. Give one advantage and one disadvantage of a potentiometer.

15.2 A student connects a potentiometer across a 6 V supply and adjusts it to give an output voltage, measured with a digital voltmeter, of 1.5 V. He then connects a 1.5 V torch bulb across the output and is very surprised when it only glows dimly. Explain why this happens.

15.3 The circuit diagram shows a 12 V battery connected across a potential divider circuit consisting of three resistors in series. Calculate the reading given by a digital voltmeter connected across BC. What would be the reading of an analogue voltmeter of resistance 6 kΩ used in place of the digital voltmeter? If both voltmeters were connected in parallel across BC at the same time, what would be the reading on each voltmeter?

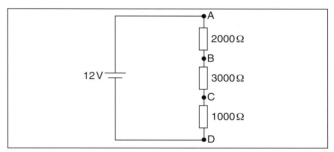

15.4 The circuit diagram shows a 4 V battery connected across a potential divider. What must happen to the output terminals to produce the maximum output current? Given that the output current must not exceed 0.5 A, calculate the resistance of R_1. The output potential difference V_{out} is found to be 3 V when the output current is 0.1 A. Calculate the resistance of R_2.

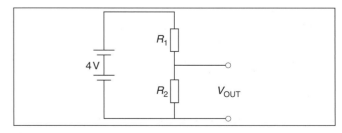

15.5 A light-dependent resistor is connected in series with a 900 Ω fixed resistor and a 5 V supply. The graph shows how the resistance of the LDR varies with the intensity (measured in lux) of the light falling on it. Using the graph, calculate the voltage across the 900 Ω resistor when the LDR is placed (a) in bright sunlight (1000 lux), (b) 50 cm away from a 40 W bulb (90 lux).

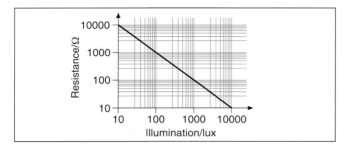

Chapter 16

16.1 State Ohm's law. Describe an experiment to test whether a conductor obeys Ohm's law.

16.2 Discuss the extent to which the tungsten filament of a lamp is ohmic.

16.3 The graph shows the current–voltage characteristics for the diode in the circuit. The cell has an e.m.f. of 2.5 V. When S is closed, the current is 50 mA. Use the graph to find the p.d. across the diode at this current. From this calculate the p.d. across R_1 and the resistance of R_1. When S is open, the current is 10 mA. Calculate R_2. Calculate the power dissipated in the diode when the switch S is closed.

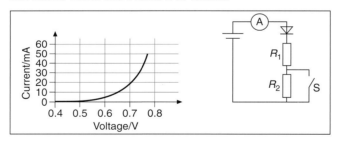

16.4 The operating voltage for a certain type of light emitting diode is 1.7 V and it needs a current of 20 mA to achieve full brightness. Calculate the value of the series resistor that has to be used when this LED is powered from a 6 V supply.

16.5 Sketch a graph showing how the resistance of an NTC thermistor varies with the potential difference across it.

Chapter 17

17.1 A battery has an e.m.f. of 9 V and drives a current of 500 mA through a resistance of 12 Ω. Calculate the voltage across the resistance and hence the battery's internal resistance.

17.2 Describe how you would measure the internal resistance of a battery.

17.3 The table contains data from an experiment to measure the internal resistance of a cell.

Current/mA	100	200	300	400	500	600
Terminal voltage/V	1.48	1.32	1.15	0.99	0.83	0.67

Use a graph of terminal voltage against current to find the e.m.f. and the internal resistance of the cell.

17.4 A small torch bulb is rated at 3.5 V, 0.35 A. Find its working resistance. Calculate the value of the series resistance needed for the bulb to operate normally from a 12 V supply with an internal resistance of 4 Ω. The same bulb operates normally when connected directly across another supply that has an e.m.f. of 4.5 V. Calculate the internal resistance of this supply.

17.5 The battery in the circuit has an e.m.f. of 12 V and an internal resistance of 2 Ω. What is the reading on the digital voltmeter with switch S open? The switch is now closed. Calculate the current flowing through the 4 Ω resistor. Find the terminal voltage of the supply. Calculate the power dissipated in the internal resistance and the power dissipated in the external circuit.

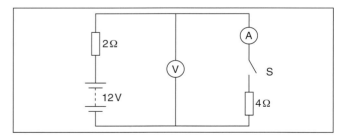

17.6 State and explain one situation where an extremely small internal resistance is desirable and one where a very large one is preferred.

Chapter 18

18.1 Define pressure. The unit of pressure is the pascal (Pa). Express this unit in terms of only base units.

18.2 This hydraulic jack has a large circular piston of radius 96 cm and a circular plunger of radius 6 cm. Calculate (a) the upward force exerted on the piston when a force of 150 N is used to push the plunger down, (b) the distance that the piston moves up when the plunger moves down 64 cm.

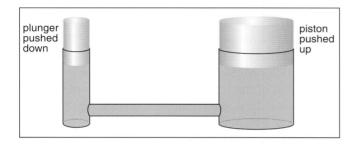

18.3 Describe a simple experiment to show that the pressure exerted by a gas in a sealed container increases with temperature. How would you need to improve your experiment to allow a full investigation of the way in which the pressure changes with temperature?

18.4 A certain thermocouple generates an e.m.f. of 35 μV for every 1 °C of the temperature difference between its two junctions. It has a resistance of 4 Ω and is connected across a very sensitive ammeter that has a resistance of 16 Ω. Calculate the current flowing through the ammeter and the power produced by the thermocouple when the temperature difference across its junctions is 160 °C.

18.5 Describe how you would calibrate a liquid-in-glass thermometer. The alcohol level in an uncalibrated alcohol-in-glass thermometer is 2.0 cm above its bulb when the thermometer is placed in melting ice and 18.0 cm above its bulb when in pure, boiling water at atmospheric pressure. Calculate how far the alcohol level will be from the bulb when the thermometer is at a temperature of (a) 35 °C, (b) –8 °C.

Chapter 19

19.1 What does macroscopic mean? State the three macroscopic properties of a gas and give their units. Name the fourth property of a gas on which these three depend.

19.2 State Boyle's law. Describe how you would demonstrate this law. Include any precautions that you would take.

19.3 Sketch the pressure–volume graph for a fixed mass of gas at constant temperature. Add to your graph a second isothermal curve representing the behaviour of the same mass of gas after it has been heated to a higher constant temperature.

19.4 A gas cylinder, volume 0.06 m³, contains air at a pressure of 1.8 MPa. The tap of the cylinder is opened and the air escapes into the atmosphere. Given that atmospheric pressure is 100 kPa, calculate the volume of air (measured at atmospheric pressure) that leaves the cylinder.

19.5 A fish resting on the bottom of a lake releases a small air bubble from its mouth. The bubble increases in volume as it journeys to the surface through water known to be at a constant temperature. Explain why the volume of the bubble increases as it rises to the surface. The volume of the released bubble was 4 mm³ but had increased to 20 mm³ by the time it had reached the surface. Given that the atmospheric pressure acting on the surface of the lake is equivalent to an additional 10 m of water, calculate the depth of the lake at the point where the fish is resting. Explain your working.

Chapter 20

20.1 State the pressure law. Describe how you would demonstrate this law. Include any precautions that you would take.

20.2 The table contains corresponding readings of temperature and pressure recorded for a fixed mass of gas maintained at a constant volume.

Temperature/°C	1	12	29	34	58	78
Pressure/kPa	96	100	106	111	116	123

Unfortunately, one of the temperature readings has been recorded incorrectly. Find out which one. Use all the other data to determine the correct value for this temperature. Show all your working.

20.3 A bottle has its cork inserted when the air pressure is 100 kPa and the temperature is 15 °C. The temperature of the bottle is then gradually increased. The cork blows out when the pressure of the air inside the bottle exceeds atmospheric pressure by 20 kPa. Calculate the temperature, in °C, at which this happens.

PRACTICE QUESTIONS

20.4 A fixed mass of gas has an initial volume V_0 and an initial pressure p_0. It is first compressed at a constant temperature of 27 °C until its volume is reduced to $\frac{1}{4}V_0$. State the pressure of the gas, in terms of p_0, at the end of this process. The temperature of the gas is now increased until its volume returns to V_0. Throughout this process, the gas is allowed to expand in such a way that its pressure remains constant. Calculate the final temperature, in °C, of the gas. Illustrate these two changes on a graph of pressure against volume. Describe the third change that is required to complete the 'cycle' of changes, i.e. to return the gas to its original conditions.

20.5 Explain the terms *critical temperature* and *ideal gas*. The ideal gas equation can be written as $pV = nRT$. State the meaning of each symbol and give its unit.

Chapter 21

21.1 Describe an experimental arrangement for observing the Brownian motion of smoke particles suspended in air. State what is observed.

21.2 Explain how the rapid, random motion of gas particles can produce Brownian motion of smoke particles in air.

21.3 Describe how the ball bearing model of a gas (Figure 21.3 in Chapter 21) can be adjusted to represent an increase in (a) the mass of gas present, (b) the temperature of the gas, (c) the pressure acting on the gas. How can such a model be used to illustrate Brownian motion?

21.4 Explain how the random motion of gas particles accounts for the pressure exerted by a gas on the walls of its container. Why does the pressure increase with increasing temperature and why does it decrease with increasing volume?

21.5 Explain what would happen if the collisions made by gas molecules were inelastic.

Chapter 22

22.1 A steady stream of balls, each of mass 0.2 kg, hits a vertical wall at right angles. The speed of the balls is 15 m s^{-1} and 600 hit the wall in 12 s. Assuming that the balls rebound at the same speed, calculate the total change of momentum and hence the average force acting on the wall during this period of time. Sketch a

graph to show how the actual force on the wall varies with time over a period of 100 ms (assume that the force changes in a linear way during each individual collision). Explain how the average force acting on the wall can be obtained from your graph.

22.2 The pressure exerted by an ideal gas can be written in the form: $p = \frac{1}{3} \rho <c^2>$. What does each symbol represent? Show that the equation is homogeneous with respect to its units. State four of the assumptions that are made about an ideal gas when deriving this equation.

22.3 The density of hydrogen gas at a pressure of 101 kPa and a temperature of 0 °C is 90 g m^{-3}. Calculate the root mean square speed of its molecules under these conditions. Sketch a graph showing the distribution of the speeds of the hydrogen molecules. On the same axes, sketch the new distribution for the same gas at a higher temperature.

22.4 The mean kinetic energy of a gas molecule is given by the equation $\frac{1}{2} mv^2 = \frac{3}{2}kT$ where k is the gas constant per molecule, known as the Boltzmann constant (1.38 × 10^{-23} J K^{-1}). (a) Show that the equation is homogeneous with respect to its units. (b) State the relationship between the Boltzmann, the Avogadro and the molar gas constants. (c) The root mean square speed of the molecules of a gas is 380 m s^{-1} at a temperature of 7 °C. Calculate their root mean square speed at a temperature of 847 °C.

22.5 Eight gas molecules are moving along the same line with the following velocities (measured in m s^{-1}): 350, 420, −280, 610, −680, −540, 590, −490. Calculate (a) the mean speed of these molecules, (b) the mean velocity, (c) the mean square speed, (d) the mean square velocity, (e) the root mean square speed, (f) the root mean square velocity.

Chapter 23

23.1 What is the internal energy of a body? Give examples of how internal energy may be increased.

23.2 Describe the motion of the molecules in a solid, a liquid and a gas. For each, explain how the substance can store internal energy.

23.3 Compare the internal energies and the temperatures of a spoonful of hot water and a bucketful of cold water.

23.4 A hot body is placed next to a cold body. Explain

why there is a net flow of energy from hot to cold if energy moves randomly between the two bodies.

23.5 Explain the difference between the internal energies of an ideal monatomic gas and a real monatomic gas.

Chapter 24

24.1 Good electrical conductors such as copper are also good thermal conductors, although the reverse is not always correct. For instance, quartz is a good conductor of heat but a very poor conductor of electricity. These statements support the fact that two possible mechanisms exist by which heat can be conducted through a solid. Describe these two mechanisms with reference to both copper and quartz.

24.2 Describe in detail how energy gets from the flame of a gas cooker to the contents of a pan of water above the flame.

24.3 A central heating system uses hot water circulating through 'radiators' to heat the rooms of a house. Describe how the energy gets from the hot water and into the room. Why doesn't the temperature of a heated room continually increase?

24.4 For each of conduction, convection and radiation, describe one situation in which it is helpful, and one situation in which it is unhelpful.

24.5 What is meant when two bodies are said to be in thermal equilibrium? Is thermal equilibrium a dynamic or static situation? Explain your answer. How does thermal equilibrium differ from steady state?

Chapter 25

25.1 Define the specific heat capacity of a material and state its unit. Express this unit in terms of only base units.

25.2 Describe how you would find the specific heat capacity of an unknown metal in the form of a block by an electrical heating method. Include a circuit diagram in your answer along with any precautions taken. Show how the specific heat capacity of the metal is calculated from your results.

25.3 A thermally insulated coil of copper wire, resistance 25 Ω and mass 30 g, has a potential difference of 5.0 V applied across its ends. Calculate the temperature rise produced in 1 minute.

25.4 The braking system on each of the four wheels of a car consists of a metal disc attached to the wheel and a pad attached to the framework of the car. During braking the pads grip the discs so that the car slows down. Each disc has a mass of 2.8 kg and its metal has a specific heat capacity of 460 J kg^{-1} K^{-1}. Calculate an approximate value for the temperature rise of each disc when the car, mass 900 kg, brakes and stops from an initial speed of 30 m s^{-1}. A single disc is removed from the car. Describe how you would measure its specific heat capacity.

25.5 Find out the atomic masses of aluminium, copper, iron and lead. Show that the specific heat capacities for these four materials are roughly inversely proportional to their atomic masses. Explain the physical reason for this. Give two reasons why concrete, which has a lower specific heat capacity than water, is regularly used instead of it to store energy?

Chapter 26

26.1 Describe the experiment that you would use to determine the specific latent heat of vaporisation of water by an electrical heating method. Include a circuit diagram in your answer along with any precautions taken. Show how the specific latent heat of vaporisation of water is calculated from your results.

26.2 The specific latent heat of vaporisation of water is 2.25 MJ kg^{-1}. Calculate the energy required to change 16 g of boiling water into steam. An electric heater decreases the mass of boiling water in an insulated container by 16 g in 1 minute. Find the minimum power of this heater. Why is its actual power likely to be greater?

26.3 An automatic electric kettle operates at a potential difference of 230 V and a current of 8 A. It is used to heat 600 g of water and itself from an initial temperature of 15 °C. The specific heat capacity of water is 4.2 kJ kg^{-1} K^{-1} and the kettle itself requires 350 J for every 1 °C rise in its temperature. Assuming that there are no energy losses and no evaporation takes place, calculate the time taken to bring the water to the boil. The automatic cut-off fails to function. The kettle is manually turned off 2 minutes after the water began to boil. How much water will be left in the kettle?

26.4 Half a pint (284 ml, equivalent to a mass of 284 g) of water in a glass has a temperature of 22 °C. Cubes of ice at a temperature of 0 °C are put into the drink to

PRACTICE QUESTIONS

cool it. Calculate (a) the energy given out by the water as it cools to 0 °C, (b) the mass of ice that melts, assuming that all the energy given out by the water is used to melt the ice. (The specific heat capacity of water is 4200 J kg^{-1} K^{-1}. The specific latent heat of fusion of ice is 330 kJ kg^{-1}.)

26.5 Three kilograms of molten lead at an initial temperature of 608 K are allowed to cool down. The temperature takes 16 s to decrease to 600 K and then remains at this value for 5 minutes. It then decreases by a further 6 K in the next 10 s. The rate at which the lead loses energy to its surroundings can be taken to be uniform throughout this period as its temperature remains fairly constant. Sketch a temperature–time graph for this cooling and state what has happened to the lead during this period of time. The specific heat capacity of solid lead is 130 J kg^{-1} K^{-1} . Find (a) the rate of loss of energy from the lead, (b) the specific latent heat of fusion of lead, (c) the specific heat capacity of molten lead.

Chapter 27

27.1 Working and heating are two processes that can increase the internal energy of an object. In what ways do they differ? Describe and explain two different ways of working on an object.

27.2 Calculate the kinetic energy of the head (mass 0.3 kg) of a hammer travelling at 15 m s^{-1}. Fifty blows from this hammer land at this speed on a piece of lead of mass 0.15 kg. At the end the lead is hot, and the hammer is still cold. Explain how the hammer can raise the temperature of the block without heating it. Calculate the total energy transferred to the lead block and its maximum temperature rise (specific heat capacity of lead is 130 J kg^{-1} K^{-1}).

27.3 A cold cell can transfer energy to a hot lamp filament. Explain why this process must be working and not heating.

27.4 A copper wire is 2.0 m long and has a cross-sectional area of 1.0 mm^2. It has a potential difference of 0.12 V across it when the current in it is 3.5 A. Calculate the electrical work done on the wire in 30 s by the power supply. Copper has about 1.7×10^{29} carrier electrons per metre cubed. Show that the drift speed of these electrons is about 0.13 mm s^{-1}. How far, on average, do these electrons move in 30 s? Hence, find the total force exerted on the electrons in the wire by the power supply.

27.5 Explain why the electric mains supply works on an electric fire rather than heats it. How does the energy then get from the fire to the room?

Chapter 28

28.1 The first law of thermodynamics can be stated in the form of the equation $\Delta U = \Delta Q + \Delta W$. Explain the meaning of each of the terms in this equation. What important principle of physics does this equation embrace?

28.2 Give two situations in which the energy transferred by heating (ΔQ) is zero.

28.3 Tea or coffee is sometimes kept hot in a thermos flask. Why does it cool down over a period of a few hours? Discuss the feasibility of ever achieving a completely isolated system.

28.4 A 24 W filament lamp has been switched on for some time. The equation $\Delta U = \Delta Q + \Delta W$ can be applied to its operation. For the next five seconds of its operation, state and explain the value of each of the terms in this equation.

28.5 An expanding gas does work as it pushes back its surroundings. With reference to the equation $\Delta U = \Delta Q + \Delta W$, explain what happens to the temperature of a rapidly expanding gas.

Chapter 29

29.1 What is a heat engine? Sketch a block diagram of a thermal power station and use this to illustrate how it makes use of a heat engine.

29.2 Define efficiency. A 60 W light bulb is 2% efficient as a light source. How much power does it give out as light? What happens to the rest of the input?

29.3 What steps would you take to make the maximum efficiency of a heat engine as large as possible? A thermocouple has two junctions at 400 °C and 27 °C respectively. Calculate its maximum possible efficiency.

29.4 How does a heat pump differ from a heat engine? Name three devices that make use of a heat pump.

29.5 The Sun's internal temperature is 5 000 000 K. The average temperature of the universe is about 3 K. Calculate the maximum efficiency of a heat engine operating between these temperatures. Explain why this efficiency will not remain at this very high value forever.

Assessment questions

1 Classify each of the terms in the left-hand column by placing a tick in the relevant box.

	Base unit	Derived unit	Base quantity	Derived quantity
Mass				
Charge				
Joule				
Ampere				
Volt				

(Total 5 marks)

(Edexcel GCE Physics Unit Test PHY2, January 2002)

2 The table gives four word equations. Complete the table with the quantity defined by each word equation.

Word equation	Quantity defined
voltage ÷ current	
voltage × current	
charge ÷ time	
work done ÷ charge	

(Total 4 marks)

(Edexcel GCE Physics Unit Test PHY2, June 2002)

3 Complete each of the following statements in words:

The resistance of an ammeter is assumed to be
....

The resistance of a voltmeter is assumed to be
.... **[2]**

Calculate the total resistance of four 5.0 Ω resistors connected in parallel. **[2]**

(Total 4 marks)

(Edexcel GCE Physics Unit Test PHY2, January 2002)

4 Three resistors of resistances R_1, R_2 and R_3 are connected in parallel with each other. They could

be replaced by a single resistor as shown.

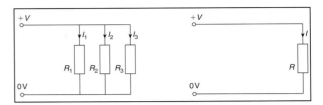

Show that the resistance, R, of the equivalent single resistor can be calculated from

$$\frac{1}{R} = \frac{1}{R_1} + \frac{1}{R_2} + \frac{1}{R_3}$$ **[3]**

A student has four identical resistors each of resistance 10 Ω. She connects them to form the three different networks shown below.

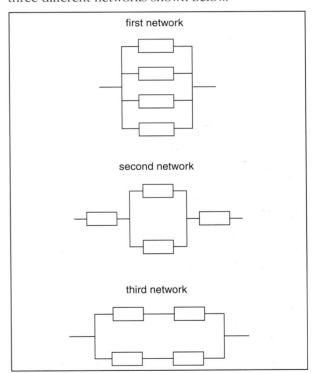

first network

second network

third network

Calculate the equivalent total resistance of each network. **[3]**

She then connects a battery across the second network and adds meters to make the circuit shown below. A current of 50 mA is drawn from the battery.

ASSESSMENT QUESTIONS

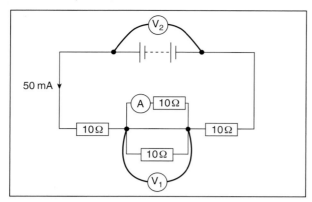

Determine the readings on the ammeter A and voltmeters V_1 and V_2. **[5]**

(Total 11 marks)
(Edexcel GCE Physics Unit Test PHY2, June 2002)

5 A negative temperature coefficient thermistor is used in the following circuit to make a temperature sensor.

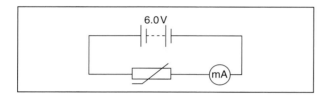

Explain how the circuit works. **[2]**

The graph shows how the resistance of the thermistor varies with temperature.

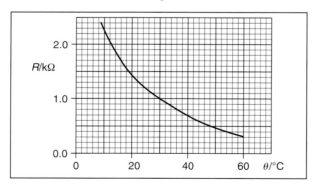

What will the reading on the milliammeter be when the thermistor is at a temperature of 20 °C? **[3]**

(Total 5 marks)
(Edexcel GCE Physics Unit Test PHY2, January 2002)

6 A copper wire has a cross-sectional area of 0.20×10^{-6} m². Copper has 1.0×10^{29} free electrons per cubic metre. Calculate the current through the wire when the drift speed of the electrons is 0.94 mm s⁻¹. **[3]**

The wire is 4.0 m long. Copper has a resistivity of 1.7×10^{-8} Ω m. Calculate the resistance of the wire. **[3]**

Calculate the potential difference across the wire. **[1]**

A second wire with the same diameter is made from a material that has a greater resistivity than copper. Explain how, if at all, the current will differ from that in the copper wire when the same p.d. is applied across it. **[2]**

The number of free electrons per cubic metre in this wire is the same as that in the copper wire. Compare the drift velocities of the free electrons in the two wires. **[1]**

(Total 10 marks)
(Edexcel GCE Physics Unit Test PHY2, January 2002)

7 A lightning stroke passes between a cloud and a lightning conductor attached to a tall building. A very large current of 20 000 A passes for 4.0×10^{-4} s.

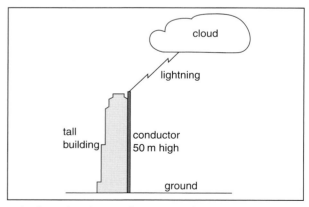

Calculate the charge flowing to the ground in this time. **[2]**

The lightning conductor is 50 m high and has a cross-sectional area of 1.0×10^{-3} m². It is made from copper, which has a resistivity of

$1.7 \times 10^{-8} \ \Omega$ m. Calculate the resistance of the lightning conductor. **[3]**

Hence calculate the potential difference between the top and bottom of the current-carrying lightning conductor. **[2]**

If lightning strikes a tree such that there is the same current through it as there was through the lightning conductor, then a much larger potential difference exists between the top and bottom of the tree. Explain why this is so. **[1]**

(Total 8 marks)
(Edexcel GCE Physics Unit Test PHY2, June 2002)

8   Two resistors of resistance 2.0 MΩ and 4.0 Ω are connected in series across a supply voltage of 6.0 V. Together they form a simple potential divider circuit.

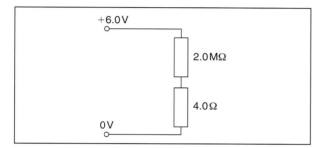

State the potential difference across each resistor.
[2]

A second potential divider circuit uses a resistor and a diode connected in series with the same supply.

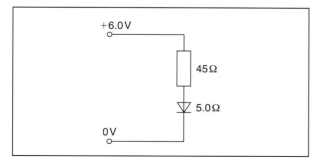

Calculate the potential difference across each component when the resistance of the resistor and diode are 45 Ω and 5.0 Ω respectively. **[2]**

In the above circuit the diode is in forward bias.

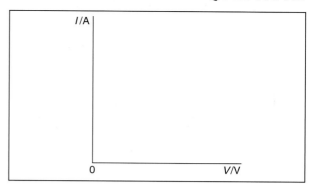

Use the axes to sketch a graph of current I against potential difference V for a diode in forward bias.
[1]

(Total 5 marks)
(Edexcel GCE Physics Unit Test PHY2, June 2002)

9   A student wants to determine the e.m.f. ε of a cell and its internal resistance r. He uses the circuit shown and measures the terminal voltage V across the cell and the current I in the circuit for each setting of the variable resistor.

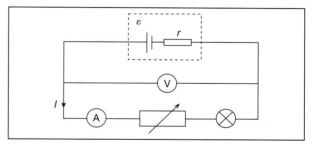

He plots the following graph of terminal voltage V against current I.

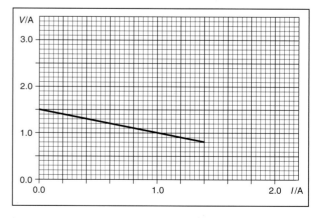

Show how the relationship $V = \varepsilon - Ir$ can be used with his graph to determine the e.m.f. ε of the cell and state its value. **[2]**

Show how the graph can be used to determine the internal resistance *r* of the cell and calculate its value. **[2]**

The student repeats the experiment using two of these cells in series. On the graph, draw the line that he obtains. **[3]**

Suggest why the student includes the filament lamp in the circuit. **[2]**

(Total 9 marks)
(Edexcel GCE Physics Unit Test PHY2, January 2002)

10 A car of weight 12 000 N is stationary on a horizontal road. The four wheels of the car are fitted with air-filled (pneumatic) tyres. The pressure of the air in each tyre is 3.0×10^5 N m^{-2}. Estimate the area of contact between each tyre and the road surface. **[2]**

The rubber in the tyres is repeatedly stretched and relaxed when the car is in motion but the overall volume of the tyres remains constant. During a journey the temperature of the air in the tyres rises from 10 °C to 30 °C. Calculate the pressure of the air at 30 °C. **[3]**

Sketch a graph to show how the area of contact between a tyre and the road varies with the pressure of the air. **[3]**

(Total 8 marks)
(Edexcel GCE Physics Unit Test PHY2, June 2002)

11 If you want to investigate how the pressure of a gas depends on the volume of the gas, two variables must be kept constant. What are they? **[2]**

Draw a labelled diagram of the apparatus you would use. **[3]**

How would you process the readings you have taken in order to produce the graph shown below?

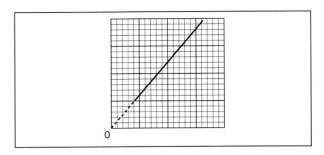

Label both axes on the graph. **[2]**

(Total 7 marks)
(Edexcel GCE Physics Unit Test PHY2, January 2002)

12 The kinetic theory of gases is based on a number of assumptions. Two of these are stated below.

First assumption: The molecules are in continuous, random motion.

Second assumption: The average distance between the molecules is much larger than the molecular diameter.

State and explain one observation which supports each assumption. **[2,2]**

(Total 4 marks)
(Edexcel GCE Physics Unit Test PHY2, June 2002)

13 A heater, for use outdoors, uses bottled gas to make a metal grill red hot. The metal grill is mounted beneath a polished aluminium hood.

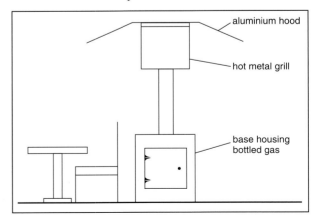

Briefly explain the advantage of having an aluminium hood which is polished on the underside and also on its upper surface. **[4]**

The bottled gas provides energy for approximately 16 hours when working at 14.4 kW power. Show that the total energy provided during this time is about 800 MJ. **[3]**

This device is 45% efficient at heating the seating area. Calculated the wasted energy. **[3]**

Explain why the efficiency of the heater will be less than 45% when it is first switched on. **[2]**

(Total 12 marks)
(Edexcel GCE Physics Unit Test PHY2, January 2002)

14 Water in a plastic kettle is heated by an electric element near the bottom of the kettle. The temperature of the water near its surface can be recorded on a thermometer.

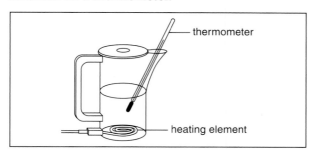

A kettle contains 0.70 kg of water at an initial temperature of 20 °C. It is calculated that about 250 kJ of thermal energy is needed to heat the water from 20 °C to 100 °C. Show how this value is calculated. (The specific heat capacity of water is 4200 J kg^{-1} K^{-1}.) **[2]**

Calculate the time it should take for an element rated at 2.2 kW to supply this energy. **[3]**

To check this calculation, the kettle is switched on at $t = 0$ s and temperature readings are taken as the water is heated. The graph shows how the temperature varies with time.

Use the graph to fully describe qualitatively how the temperature of the water changes during the first 160 s. **[3]**

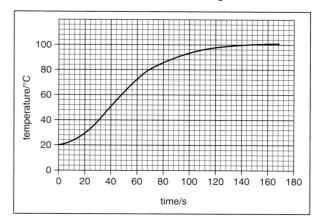

Estimate the efficiency of the electric heating element in bringing the water to the boil. **[2]**

(Total 10 marks)
(Edexcel GCE Physics Unit Test PHY2, June 2002)

15 The contents of a domestic refrigerator are at a constant temperature of 5 °C, and the outside surface of the refrigerator is at a constant temperature of 20 °C.

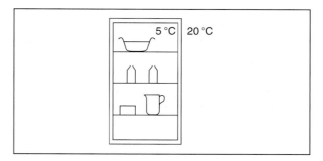

Explain how it is possible for the contents of the refrigerator to be at a constant temperature even though energy is continuously flowing in from outside. You may be awarded a mark for the clarity of your answer. **[3]**

The equation $\Delta U = \Delta Q + \Delta W$ can be applied to the contents of the refrigerator.

What is the value of ΔU? Explain your answer. **[2]**

What is meant by ΔQ in this equation? **[2]**

Explain why ΔW is zero. **[1]**

(Total 8 marks)
(Edexcel GCE Physics Unit Test PHY2, January 2002)

ASSESSMENT QUESTIONS

16 A Smoke Jack is an example of an 18th century heat engine that was found in the large kitchens of manor houses and stately homes. It consists of four rotating paddles, which are in the chimney, directly above the open log fire. The paddles are connected to the spit by gears and pulleys. Food on the spit is slowly cooked as the spit rotates. A diagram of a simple Smoke Jack is shown below.

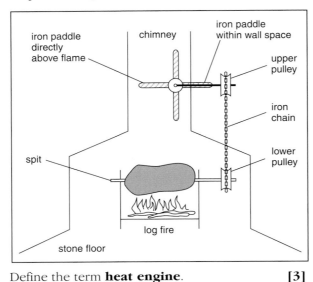

Define the term **heat engine**. [3]

During a cold winter, the temperature of the air at the top of the chimney is −5 °C and that of the hot air just above the flames is at 350 °C. Calculate the maximum thermal efficiency of this Smoke Jack. [3]

In practice, the Smoke Jack's thermal efficiency is much less than this. With reference to the diagram state two different ways by which the thermal energy from the logs would be wasted. [2]

The molecules of the gases in the air are in constant random motion and so possess random kinetic energy. It can be assumed that these gases behave as ideal gases. Hence calculate the ratio of the average kinetic energy of the molecules just above the flames to that of the molecules at the top of the chimney. [2]

(Total 10 marks)
(Edexcel GCE Physics Unit Test PHY2, June 2002)

Topic Questions

Topic A – Astrophysics

A1 State two advantages of positioning an optical telescope on the top of a mountain. [2]

(Total 2 marks)
(Edexcel GCE Physics Unit Test PHY3, June 2002, part question)

A2 State two similarities and one difference between light and radio waves. [3]

(Total 3 marks)
(Edexcel GCE Physics Unit Test PHY3, January 2002, part question)

A3 Stars β Ori and α Cet have temperatures of approximately 11 000 K and 3600 K respectively. Calculate the wavelength at which the intensity of radiation from each star is a maximum. Give your answers in nanometres. [3]

Use the Stefan–Boltzmann law to calculate the power emitted per square metre of surface, measured in $W\,m^{-2}$, for β Ori. [2]

The power emitted per square metre of surface for α Cet = $1.0 \times 10^7\ W\,m^{-2}$. Sketch two graphs on the axes below, showing how this emitted power is distributed over different wavelengths for each star.

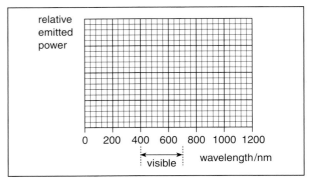

Label your graphs Ori and Cet. [3]

The visible spectrum extends from approximately 400 nm to 700 nm. Use your graphs to explain why β Ori is a bluish star, while α Cet is reddish. [2]

(Total 10 marks)
(Edexcel GCE Physics Unit Test PHY3, January 2002, part question)

A4 Explain why the term **light year** is a measure of distance and not of time. **[1]**

Show that the light year is equivalent to a distance of approximately 9×10^{15} m. **[2]**

Draw a labelled diagram to illustrate the principle of how the distance to a nearby star can be measured using the annual parallax method. **[4]**

Why is this method only suitable for nearby stars? **[1]**

(Total 8 marks)

(Edexcel GCE Physics Unit Test PHY3, January and June 2002, combined part questions)

A5 The table shows the properties of three stars.

	Star	Luminosity/$L_\odot$	Temperature/K
A	α Ori	6×10^4	3500
B	Procy B	3×10^{-4}	7000
C	β Per	2×10^2	12 000

On the Hertzsprung–Russell diagram below, mark with an x_A, x_B and x_C the approximate position of each of the three stars. **[1]**

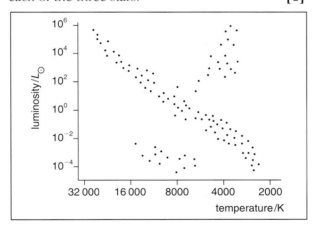

State whether each star is a main sequence star, a red giant or a white dwarf. **[3]**

Use the Stefan–Boltzmann law to calculate the surface area and hence the radius of α Ori. (Luminosity of the Sun = 3.8×10^{26} W.) **[5]**

(Total 9 marks)

(Edexcel GCE Physics Unit Test PHY3, June 2002, part question)

A6 What is a supernova? Describe briefly what happens during the formation of a supernova. You may be awarded a mark for the clarity of your answer. **[5]**

What are the two possible fates for the central core remnant from a supernova explosion? **[2]**

(Total 7 marks)

(Edexcel GCE Physics Unit Test PHY3, June 2002, part question)

Topic B – Solid Materials

B1 Calculate the stress in a steel wire of length 2.6 m and cross-sectional area 1.5×10^{-7} m² when it is subjected to a tensile force of 8.0 N. **[2]**

Part of a force–extension graph for such a steel wire is shown below.

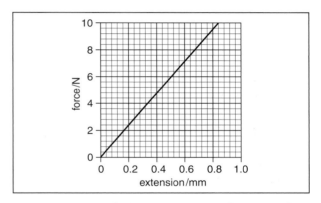

Use the graph to find the extension of the wire for an applied force of 8.0 N. Show that the corresponding strain in the wire is approximately 3×10^{-4}. Hence determine the Young modulus for steel. **[4]**

Calculate the work done in stretching the wire by 0.4 mm. **[3]**

A second wire is made of the same steel. It has the same cross-sectional area but twice the length. On the same axes draw the force–extension graph for this wire. **[2]**

(Total 11 marks)

(Edexcel GCE Physics Unit Test PHY3, June 2002, part question)

ASSESSMENT QUESTIONS

B2 Some properties of two materials A and B are given below, material A on the graph, material B in the table.

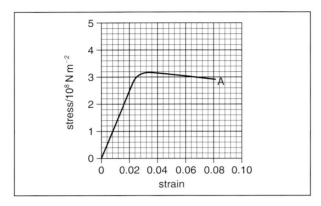

Material	Young modulus/ 10^{10} Pa	Ultimate tensile stress/ 10^8 N m^{-2}	Nature
A			Tough
B	3.0	3.6	Brittle

Use the graph to complete the table for material A. **[2]**

Use the table to draw a graph on the grid above showing the behaviour of material B. **[3]**

Show on the graph the region in which material A obeys Hooke's law. **[1]**

Material A is in the form of a wire of cross-sectional area 8.8×10^{-7} m^2 and length 2.5 m. Calculate the energy stored in the wire when it experiences a strain of 0.020. **[4]**

(Total 10 marks)
(Edexcel GCE Physics Unit Test PHY3, January 2002, part question)

B3 The photograph is of a bubble raft model of an edge dislocation.

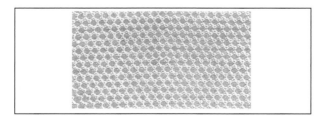

What do the bubbles represent? **[1]**

Indicate on the photograph where the "dislocation" in the bubble raft occurs. **[1]**

(Total 2 marks)
(Edexcel GCE Physics Unit Test PHY3, June 2002, part question)

B4 A horizontal concrete beam rests on two pillars, one at each end, forming a bridge. It supports a large load at its centre. Draw the concrete beam and show the regions of the beam which are in tension and the regions which are in compression. **[2]**

Explain why microscopic cracks in the lower surface of the beam are more dangerous than any which form in the upper surface of the beam. You may be awarded a mark for the clarity of your answer. **[3]**

(Total 5 marks)
(Edexcel GCE Physics Unit Test PHY3, June 2002, part question)

B5 Perspex is an amorphous polymer. Draw a labelled diagram showing the molecular structure of Perspex. **[2]**

Describe the difference in behaviour of a thermoplastic polymer and a thermosetting polymer when heated. **[2]**

Is Perspex a thermoplastic polymer or a thermosetting polymer? **[1]**

(Total 5 marks)
(Edexcel GCE Physics Unit Test PHY3, January 2002, part question)

B6 The table gives the properties of three different materials.

	Ultimate tensile stress/10^6 N m^{-2}	Young modulus/ 10^9 Pa
A	0.7	30
B	100	2
C	650	40

Use this data to describe each material as either strong or weak and either stiff or flexible. **[3]**

The materials are CFRP (carbon fibre reinforced polymer), nylon and polythene. Identify materials A, B and C. **[2]**

State which of these materials is/are a composite material(s). **[1]**

(Total 6 marks)

(Edexcel GCE Physics Unit Test PHY3, June 2002, part question)

B7 Describe the difference between a fibre composite and a laminate. **[2]**

Explain how the risk of failure by cracking is reduced in **either** a fibre composite **or** a laminate. You may be awarded a mark for the clarity of your answer. **[3]**

(Total 5 marks)

(Edexcel GCE Physics Unit Test PHY3, January 2002, part question)

Topic C – Nuclear and Particle Physics

C1 Show that the radius of the nucleus of an atom of silver, $^{108}_{47}$Ag, is approximately twice the radius of the nucleus of a nitrogen atom, $^{14}_{7}$N. **[3]**

(Total 3 marks)

(Edexcel GCE Physics Unit Test PHY3, January 2002, part question)

C2 State one similarity and two differences between alpha and beta particles. **[3]**

(Total 3 marks)

(Edexcel GCE Physics Unit Test PHY3, January 2002, part question)

C3 A stationary neutron can decay to a proton and an electron. Use the data below to predict the maximum total kinetic energy of the electron and the proton in MeV.
Data: mass of neutron = 1.008 665 u
mass of proton = 1.007 276 u
mass of electron = 0.000 549 u
1 u = 930 MeV **[3]**

Explain why the principle of conservation of linear momentum tells you that almost all this kinetic energy is given to the electron. **[2]**

On the axes below sketch a graph showing the energy spectrum for the β^- particles produced during beta decay.

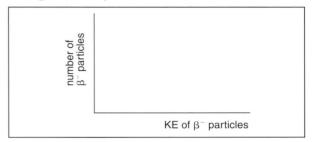

Add a scale to the horizontal axis. **[3]**

Explain why the shape of this graph led to the prediction of the existence of neutrinos. You may be awarded a mark for the clarity of your answer. **[3]**

(Total 11 marks)

(Edexcel GCE Physics Unit Test PHY3, June 2002, part question)

C4 State one similarity and one difference between a proton and an antiproton. **[2]**

Write down two particle–antiparticle pairs of leptons. **[2]**

What happens when a particle and its antiparticle collide? **[1]**

(Total 5 marks)

(Edexcel GCE Physics Unit Test PHY3, June 2002, part question)

C5 An atom of antihydrogen (a positron orbiting around an antiproton) has been produced. Is an atom of antihydrogen positive, negative or neutral? **[1]**

State the quark composition of an antiproton. **[1]**

Show that an antiproton has a charge of −1. **[1]**

Explain why it is extremely difficult to store antimatter. **[2]**

ASSESSMENT QUESTIONS

Complete the following quark table. **[1]**

Quarks			Charge
up	charm		$+\frac{2}{3}$
down	strange		$-\frac{1}{3}$

Selecting from the shaded boxes only, use the table to deduce the quark composition of (i) a neutral strange meson, (ii) a positive charmed meson, and (iii) a neutral strange baryon. **[3]**

(Total 9 marks)

(Edexcel GCE Physics Unit Test PHY3, January 2002, part question)

C6 Use the laws of conservation of charge and baryon number to decide whether the following interactions are possible or not. In each case show how you applied the laws.

(i) Δ^{++} →   p   + π^+ **[2]**
     (uuu)   (u$\bar{\text{d}}$)

(ii) Δ^- →   n   + π^- **[2]**
     (ddd)   ($\bar{\text{u}}$d)

These two decays are examples of strong interactions. What exchange particle is responsible for the decays? **[1]**

Delta particles are baryons consisting of u and d quarks only. Two more members of the delta particle family are the Δ^+ and the Δ^0. These are excited states of the proton and the neutron. State the quark composition of the Δ^+ and the Δ^0. **[2]**

(Total 7 marks)

(Edexcel GCE Physics Unit Test PHY3, June 2002, part question)

Topic D – Medical Physics

D1 A patient's thyroid function is to be investigated by means of a radionuclide tracer. Iodine accumulates in the thyroid. Which of the three isotopes of iodine listed below would be most suitable for such an investigation? **[1]**

Isotope	Mode of decay	Half-life
$^{123}_{53}\text{I}$	γ	13 hours
$^{125}_{53}\text{I}$	γ	60 days
$^{131}_{53}\text{I}$	β^- and γ	8 days

Explain why the other two isotopes would not be appropriate. **[2]**

(Total 3 marks)

(Edexcel GCE Physics Unit Test PHY3, June 2002, part question)

D2 The diagram shows the essential features of a simple gamma camera.

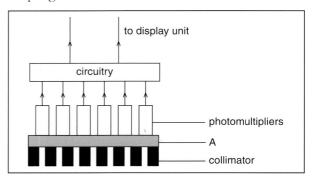

Add a label to the line marked A. **[1]**

What is the purpose of the collimator and from what material is it made? **[2]**

Describe one physical process that takes place in a photomultiplier. **[2]**

(Total 5 marks)

(Edexcel GCE Physics Unit Test PHY3, January 2002, part question)

D3 An X-ray tube operating at 65 kV has a tube current of 0.12 A. It produces X-rays with an efficiency of 0.8%. Calculate the rate of production of heat at the anode. **[3]**

What feature of the X-ray tube helps dissipate this energy? [1]

Would the X-rays produced by this tube be more suitable for diagnosis or therapy? Justify your answer. [3]

(Total 7 marks)

(Edexcel GCE Physics Unit Test PHY3, June 2002, part question)

D4 Complete the table below. [4]

X-ray use	Typical accelerating voltage	Dependence of X-ray absorption on proton number
Diagnosis		
Therapy		

When using X-rays for therapy it is important that healthy tissue receives as low a dose as possible. State and explain one way in which these low doses are achieved. [3]

(Total 7 marks)

(Edexcel GCE Physics Unit Test PHY3, January 2002, part question)

D5 Explain why high frequency ultrasound is used for scanning an eye but a lower frequency is more suitable for abdominal scans. You may be awarded a mark for the clarity of your answer. [3]

Suggest an appropriate wavelength for the ultrasound to be used in an eye investigation. Hence calculate a suitable frequency for such an investigation. (Speed of sound in water = 1.5×10^3 m s^{-1}.) [3]

During an ultrasound scan single pulses of ultrasound are transmitted at regular intervals. Typically pulses of duration 10 μs are transmitted at 120 μs intervals. On the grid below draw a scale diagram showing two consecutive pulses. [2]

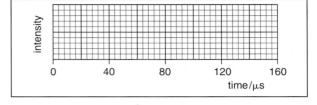

Why is it important that the pulses are well separated? [1]

(Total 9 marks)

(Edexcel GCE Physics Unit Test PHY3, June 2002, part question)

D6 The specific acoustic impedance Z of a material is calculated by multiplying its density by the speed of sound in the material. Show that Z has the units kg m^{-2} s^{-1}. [2]

Data: $Z_{air} = 400$ kg m^{-2} s^{-1}
$Z_{soft\ tissue} = 1.6 \times 10^6$ kg m^{-2} s^{-1}

Use this information to help you explain why it is impossible to use ultrasound to investigate any part of the body which is behind the lungs. You may be awarded a mark for the clarity of your answer. [5]

Give a reason why ultrasound is preferred to X-rays for examining unborn babies. [1]

(Total 8 marks)

(Edexcel GCE Physics Unit Test PHY3, January 2002, part question)

D7 State two advantages of using ultrasound for diagnosis compared with using X-rays for diagnosis. [2]

(Total 2 marks)

(Edexcel GCE Physics Unit Test PHY3, June 2002, part question)

Things you need to know

Chapter 1 What happens in an electric circuit?

charge carrier: something that moves in a circuit to make a current

cell: device for supplying electricity from two electrodes placed in chemicals

current: a flow of charge

electrical working: process in which a voltage pushes charge through a distance

battery: collection of cells connected together

direct current: electrons all flow in the same direction

Chapter 2 Charge and current

charge: quantity associated with electrical forces; like charges repel, and unlike charges attract

neutral: having an equal number of positive and negative charges resulting in no overall electrical effects

coulomb: unit of charge

current: rate of flow of charge; amp = coulomb per second

Chapter 3 Current in series circuits

shunt: device added in parallel with an ammeter to increase its range

series: components connected so that the same current goes through one and then through the next and then through the next in turn

Chapter 4 Kirchhoff's first law

parallel: components connected across each other; the voltage across each is the same; the current has a choice of routes

Kirchhoff I: the sum of the currents entering a point is equal to the sum of the currents leaving that point

Chapter 5 Controlling current

resistor: component that opposes the flow of current

light-dependent resistor: resistance decreases as level of illumination increases

thermistor: resistance which changes as the temperature changes

Chapter 7 Electrical power and energy calculations

electromotive force: voltage across a component, such as a cell or a generator, that does work on a charge

potential difference: voltage across a component, such as a resistor or a lamp, that takes energy from a charge

voltage between two points: work done moving a unit charge between two points; volt = joule per coulomb

Chapter 9 Kirchhoff's second law

voltage at a point: voltage difference between zero (0 V) and that point

voltage across a component: difference between the voltage at one end and the voltage at the other end

Kirchhoff II: around any closed loop, the sum of the e.m.f.s is equal to the sum of the p.d.s; Kirchhoff II is an electrical version of the principle of conservation of energy

Chapter 10 Resistance

resistance: property of a *component* that opposes current

dissipated: spread around

Chapter 12 How fast does charge move?

(charge) carrier density: number of charged particles per metre cubed that are free to move and carry current

drift speed (drift velocity): average rate of progress of the carriers through a circuit; very slow

Chapter 13 Resistivity

resistivity: property of a *material* which shows how well it conducts

metals: have high carrier density; reduction of drift velocity with increasing temperature decreases current flow

semiconductors: have low carrier density, which increases with increasing temperature; this allows greater current flow despite reduction of drift speed with temperature

Chapter 14 The potential divider

potential divider: chain of resistors that divides up the voltage from a source in proportion to the resistance values

Chapter 15 Controlling voltage

rheostat: variable resistor, connected in series with component, to control the current through it

potentiometer: variable potential divider used to control the voltage across a component

Chapter 16 Voltage–current characteristics

V–I characteristics: graph showing how current varies with voltage

Ohm's law: current through component is proportional to voltage across provided the temperature remains constant

ohmic: component that obeys Ohm's law: *V–I* characteristics show a straight line through the origin

diode: component that conducts easily in one (forward) direction but not in the other (reverse)

forward direction: current flows freely in this direction through a diode

reverse direction: very little current flows in this direction through a diode

Chapter 17 Internal resistance

terminal p.d.: voltage across terminals of a supply; work done on external circuit per coulomb of charge that flows

lost volts: difference between e.m.f. and terminal p.d.; voltage drop across internal resistance of supply

internal resistance: resistance to flow of current within a power supply

e.m.f.: work done by supply on both external and internal resistances per coulomb of charge that flows

Chapter 18 Pressure and temperature

rigid: something that keeps its shape

fluid: something that flows; a liquid or gas

pressure: force acting per unit area

calibrate: mark with a scale

Chapter 19 Macroscopic gas properties

macroscopic properties: large-scale gas properties that can be observed in the laboratory

isothermal: at constant temperature

Boyle's law: for a fixed mass of gas at constant temperature, pressure × volume is constant

Chapter 20 The ideal gas equation

absolute zero: the zero of the Kelvin scale of temperature (−273.15 °C); the lowest temperature theoretically possible

pressure law: for a fixed mass of gas at constant volume, the pressure is directly proportional to the Kelvin temperature

critical temperature: a gas cannot be liquefied when above its critical temperature

ideal gas: a gas that obeys the **ideal gas equation** $pV = (m/M)RT$ in all situations – it does not liquefy

constant-volume gas thermometer: an instrument for measuring Kelvin temperature

molar mass: the mass of one mole of a substance

THINGS YOU NEED TO KNOW

Chapter 21 Modelling the behaviour of a gas

Brownian motion: the random motion of visible particles caused by random impacts from invisible molecules

Chapter 22 Kinetic theory of an ideal gas

root mean square (r.m.s.) speed: the square root of the mean square speed, where the mean square speed is the sum of the squares of the molecular speeds divided by the total number of molecules

Kelvin temperature: temperature on the scale that starts at absoute zero; in °C + 273; proportional to the average molecular kinetic energy of an ideal gas

Chapter 23 Internal energy

internal energy: random kinetic and potential energy of the molecules of a body

Chapter 24 Steady state and thermal equilibrium

thermal conduction: flow of internal energy through a material without the material itself moving

convection: thermal transmission of energy as a result of the material moving and taking energy with it

thermal equilibrium: bodies at the same temperature as each other; no net energy flow thermally from one to another

heat or **heat transfer:** the energy transferred as a result of temperature difference

steady state: where all temperatures throughout a material are remaining constant, producing a steady flow of internal energy

Chapter 25 Specific heat capacity

specific heat capacity (or **specific enthalpy**): energy needed to raise the temperature of 1kg of that substance by 1K without a change of state

Chapter 26 Specific latent heat

specific latent heat of vaporisation (or **specific enthalpy of vaporisation**): energy needed to turn 1kg of liquid into vapour at a constant temperature (its boiling point)

specific latent heat of fusion (or **specific enthalpy of fusion**): energy needed to turn 1kg of solid into liquid at a constant temperature (its melting point)

Chapter 27 Heating and working

mechanical working: process in which energy transfer occurs when a force moves through a distance

heating: process in which energy transfer is driven by a temperature difference, energy flowing from hot to cold

Chapter 28 The first law of thermodynamics

first law of thermodynamics: increase in internal energy (ΔU) = energy transferred by heating (ΔQ) + energy transferred by working (ΔW)

Chapter 29 Heat engines and heat pumps

heat engine: a device that takes energy from a hot source, uses some of this to do mechanical work, and gives the rest to a cold sink

heat pump: a device that moves internal energy from a cold body to a hot body when work is done on it

efficiency: proportion of work or energy input that comes out usefully

Equations to learn

Electric current	$I = \dfrac{\Delta Q}{\Delta t}$
Energy transferred electrically	$W = IVt$
Potential difference	$V = \dfrac{W}{Q}$
Resistance	$R = \dfrac{V}{I}$
Pressure	$p = \dfrac{F}{A}$
Ideal gas equation	$pV = \left(\dfrac{m}{M}\right)RT$
	$\dfrac{p_1 V_1}{T_1} = \dfrac{p_2 V_2}{T_2}$

Index

Page references in *italics* refer to a table or an illustration.

INDEX

INDEX